# NORF
# AT WAR

# NORFOLK AT WAR

## Wings of Friendship

Frank Meeres

AMBERLEY

First published 2012

Amberley Publishing
The Hill, Stroud
Gloucestershire, GL5 4EP

www.amberley-books.com

Copyright © Frank Meeres 2012

British Library Cataloguing in Publication Data.
A catalogue record for this book is available from the British Library.

ISBN 978 1 4456 0466 4

Typeset in 10pt on 12pt Sabon.
Typesetting and Origination by Amberley Publishing.
Printed in the UK.

# Contents

# Acknowledgments

All but two of the images come from the United States Army Air Force 2nd Air Division Memorial Library Archive. I am extremely grateful to the Governors of the 2nd Air Division (USAAF) Memorial Trust for permission to use this material held at the Norfolk Record Office, which has also generously given permission for its use.

The two images not part of the American Memorial Library collection, are page 116 top, used by kind permission of Seething Control Tower; and page 109 bottom, drawn by Ludwig Lund, which is used by kind permission of his daughter Mrs Marjorie Lund-Fontaine.

The archive of the American Memorial Library has recently been catalogued with the aid of a generous grant from the Jordan Uttall/Evelyn Cohen Trust Fund: the cataloguing archivist was Ellie Jones and the project archivist Hannah Verge. This book could not have been written without their work, and also owes much to the support of Libby Morgan of the American Memorial Library.

**Images:** p. 10 MC 376/592/22; p. 13 MC 376/658; p. 18 MC 376/299/1; pp 21/22 MC 371/485; p. 26 MC 376/352; p. 27 MC 376/52; p. 29 MC 371/2; p. 32 MC 376/138; p. 33 MC 376/352; p. 35 MC 376/138; p. 38 MC 376/592/22/41; p. 41 MC 371/22; p. 42 MC 376/768/3; p. 43 MC 371/89; p. 45 MC 376/138; p. 46 MC 376/549; p. 49 MC 371/747; p. 56 MC 371/785/17; p. 60 MC 376/52; p. 64 MC 376/138; p. 66 MC 376/592, 371/485; p. 69 MC 376/466, 376/299/2; p. 70 MC 376/139/3; p. 71 MC 371/658; p. 74 MC 371/478; p. 80 MC 376/139; p. 81 MC 376/121; p. 83 MC 376/139/4, MC 376/631/1; p. 86 MC 376/485, MC 376/300/2; p. 87 MC 371/603; p. 88 MC 371/7; p. 89 MC 376/38; p. 91 MC 371/815, 376/814/2; p.92 MC 371/786/10; p. 95 MC 371/775/8; p. 96 MC 371/46; p. 97 MC 371/631; p. 98 MC 371/807; p. 100/101 MC 376/336; p. 102 MC 371/912; p. 103 MC 371/485/2; p. 105 MC 371/912/4, 376/121; p. 109 MC 371/485/1, courtesy Mrs M. Lund-Fontaine; p. 110 MC 376/139, 371/777/33; p. 113 MC 371/807/2; p. 116 NRO FX 335/1, MC 376/353/6; p. 117 MC 371/912; p. 121 MC 379/779/14; p. 122 MC 379/779/18; p. 128 MC 376/300/1; p.130/131 MC 371/912/1; p. 132 MC 371/350/8; p. 133 MC 376/179; p. 138 MC 376/299; p. 140/141 MC 371/658, 376/138, 371/485; p. 143 MC 376/350/7; p. 145 MC 376/300; p. 146 MC 371/49; p. 147 MC 376/639; p. 152/153 MC 376/184.

# Introduction

The Second World War began in September 1939 when Nazi Germany, under the rule of Adolf Hitler, invaded Poland. Britain and France declared war in Poland's support. By the summer of 1940, most of western and central Europe was under the control of Germany and her ally, Italy. In the summer and autumn of 1940, Hitler unleashed his Luftwaffe on England, with a thousand German planes a day crossing the channel. They were met by the pilots of the Royal Air Force, which included pilots from conquered nations in Europe such as Poland, Czechoslovakia and France. The Germans were driven back but invasion of Britain still seemed a very real possibility.

Only a few countries in Europe were neutral – Switzerland, Spain, Sweden and (for a time, in an uneasy alliance with Germany) the Soviet Union. Britain fought on alone, but with the countries of her Empire in support from a distance. Across the Atlantic Ocean, the United States also remained neutral, but in sympathy with Britain rather than Germany. In a *Fireside Chat* in December 1940, President Franklin Roosevelt called the States 'the great arsenal of democracy'; a resource for Britain's military needs, as well as its own.

There were dramatic changes in 1941. In June, Hitler invaded the Soviet Union. Meanwhile naval battles in the Atlantic led to American losses, most famously the *Reuben James*, sunk by German torpedoes in October, with the loss of 115 men. On 7 December 1941, the Japanese attacked the American fleet at Pearl Harbour in Honolulu. Roosevelt at once declared war upon Japan. Four days later, on 11 December 1941, Germany and Italy declared war upon the United States. The war had changed from being a European conflict to a worldwide struggle.

Hitler is supposed to have said after Pearl Harbour, 'I don't see much future for the Americans. It's a decayed country.' This was a major error. The States had great resources of people and material on which to draw, but of course it would take time to build up a force capable of liberating the continent of Europe. One alternative was to liberate North Africa first, driving out the Italian and German armies, and enter Europe from the south, but even this would involve many months of preparation: American industry had first to be converted into a war footing and men – and women – needed training.

A quicker way of bringing home the new war situation to German-occupied Europe was from the air. The Royal Air Force was bombing German cities already. They did this at night to minimise losses. America could help by delivering large bomb loads onto specific military targets during daylight hours, the large, relatively slow-moving bombers, protected from attack by German aircraft by faster fighter planes acting as escorts. Bombing aircraft factories, munitions works and oil refineries would have a direct impact on Germany's ability to wage war, and destroying bridges and railways would make it much harder for essential supplies to be transported to the front lines.

The United States 8th Air Force was established in January 1942. It was composed of three air divisions, each with fighter units and maintenance organizations to support the bomber operations. The 1st Air Division (in the Huntingdon area) and the 3rd Air Division (in Suffolk and Southwest Norfolk) were equipped with Boeing B-17 Fortress bombers. The 2nd Air Division (based in Norfolk and northeast Suffolk) evolved out of the reorganisation of VIII Bomber Command into the 8th Air Force. Starting as the 2nd Bomb Wing, it became the 2nd Bomb Division and after a fighter wing (the 65th Fighter Wing) was assigned, in September 1944, it was redesignated the 2nd Air Division in January 1945.

The plane they used was the Consolidated B-24 Liberator bomber, made by the Ford Motor Company in Michigan. In 1944 they were turning out one plane every hour, each one costing a fraction under $300,000. Four-engined heavy bombers, they were faster and lighter than the B-17, but not as well-armed. They normally had ten half-inch machine guns. The B-24 was a big plane, with a wingspan of 110 feet. Its top speed was about 300 mph, and its normal range was just over 2,000 miles. The B-24 was nicknamed the 'Ugly Duckling' by its crews, who commonly personalised their aircraft, giving them names and painting the noses with individual artwork. The crew varied from eight to ten men and would typically include the pilot, co-pilot, navigator, radio operator, engineer, bombardier and gunners.

The 44 Bomb Group (hereafter BG) arrived at Shipdham in early October 1942 – rain had turned the airfield to mud and one B-24 stuck fast after coming off the runway! The first missions were against U-Boat pens in Western France. 389 BG arrived at Hethel in June 1943, but after only two weeks flew to North Africa to join other 2nd Division groups in attacks on Sicily and then on Ploesti. 392 BG arrived at Wendling in August 1943, and began flying decoy missions over the North Sea. The first three missions, with fighter escort, passed without incident, but the fourth was unescorted and was attacked by more than thirty enemy fighters. Four planes and forty-three men were lost. Five more groups arrived between November 1943 and January 1944. They included 445 BG, which arrived at Tibenham in November to two days of glorious sunshine before winter rain set in, and 453 BG, which came to Old Buckenham in December to rain, cold winds and snow; they found the base already a quagmire. Five more groups arrived in March and April 1944. A few groups used already-established RAF bases, such as 458 BG at Horsham, but most airbases were brand new constructions.

At full strength, the 2nd Air Division had fourteen bomb groups. Each airbase was occupied by a single bomb group consisting of four flying bomb squadrons, a squadron having an average complement of twelve to sixteen B-24 aircraft and 200 combat airmen. For every one man in the air there were approximately another

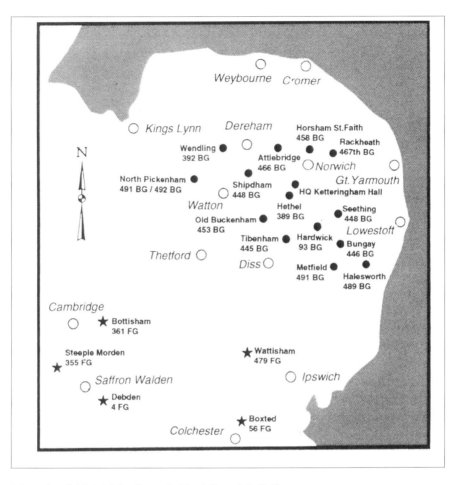

Map of 2nd Air Division bases in Norfolk and Suffolk

### 2nd Air Division Bases

| | |
|---|---|
| HQ Ketteringham Hall | 453rd Old Buckenham |
| 44th Shipdham | 458th Horsham St Faith |
| 93rd Hardwick | 466th Attlebridge |
| 389th Hethel | 467th Rackheath |
| 392nd Wendling | 489th Halesworth |
| 445th Tibenham | 491st metfield (initially) |
| 446th Bungay | 491st North Pickenham |
| 448th Seething | 492nd North Pickenham |

### Fighter groups 56th Fighter Wing

| | |
|---|---|
| 4th Debden | 361st Bottisham |
| 56th Boxted | 479th Wattisham |
| 355th Steple Morden | |

Generals W. E. Kepner and J. P. Hodges: Hodges commanded the Division between September 1942 and August 1944, Kepner between August 1944 and May 1945.

seven to ten on the ground engaged in support activities ranging from cooks, clerks, mechanics, armourers, medics, military policemen and administrators. Total personnel on a bomber station varied between two and three thousand.

This book tells the story of the experiences of these incomers, using words from their own letters and journals, and also the views that the people of East Anglia had of these 'friendly invaders'.

# Chapter One

# The Journey Across The Pond

For those who brought their planes into Britain, the choice was between the northern route and the southern. The northern was of course much colder, involving hops to Newfoundland, Greenland and Iceland: Several men noticed the unfriendly atmosphere among the German-sympathising Icelanders. **Curtis Anderson Jr** (492 BG) recalled:

Our crew was first formed early in March 1944 in Salt Lake City. We went to a bomber training base at Biggs Field, El Paso, Texas. After completing our bomber training as a crew we went to Topeka, Kansas, a staging area. There we picked up a new B-24, checked it out for a few days and then flew it to Prestwick, Scotland, by way of Bangor, Maine; Goose Bay, Labrador; and Bluie West One, Greenland.

Men taking the southern route included **Robert Boyle** (489 BG):

28 April 1944: I've covered quite a bit of ground since I left Kansas. I've flown over all kinds of country. Plains, swamps, jungles and mountains plus a lot of water, until now I am on the other side of the world in a sense. I am south of the equator, in Brazil. If all goes well I'll be in [word cut out] this time tomorrow night.

**Ernest Gavitt** (492 BG):

The crew was formed in late 1943 at Davis-Monthan Air Base in Tucson, Arizona. We took further training at Alamorgordo Air Base in New Mexico. We flew from Florida to Puerto Rico and on to Belem, Brazil, our next stop was Fortaleza and then across the ocean to Marakech [*sic*] for a day or so before a night take off, around midnight or later. We flew the 10th Meridian along the coast of Portugal by the Bay of Biscay and into St Georges Channel landing at Prestwick, then onto North Pickenham.

**Delmar Johnson** (392 BG) described the navigation techniques involved:

In our transatlantic fight we were briefed on a powerful radio beacon in Northern Ireland, but were warned to use it with caution as the Germans sometimes sent out a false signal which would lead you south of England to occupied Europe if you followed it. This would be fairly easy to do, as far out at sea the radio compass reading would be only very slightly different from the true signal. I think we were over 1,500 miles from it when, to my amazement, I was able to pick it up. I did take a check on it periodically as we flew on, and the bearing was always about as it should have been for my calculated position. However, on that trip, I relied on celestial navigation primarily, using dead reckoning based on meteorology forecast winds (in calculating drift and groundspeed) between celestial 'fixes'. I recall taking a celestial fix shortly before we were due to fly in clouds (per meteorology forecast) for awhile and another shortly before daybreak ... After the sun was a ways above the horizon, I took a couple of observations of it, probably about an hour apart. Since it was nearly directly ahead, the resulting LOP [line of position] was at right angles to our course and served as an excellent 'speed line', i.e. showed how much distance we had covered in the interval between observations, and thus permitted an accurate calculation of our ground speed. Our landfall proved to be within about a minute and a couple or so miles of my last estimate.

Most of the men came in troopships. Some soldiers were cautious of censorship rules such as **Alfred Ronald Neumunz** (453 BG), who wrote to his girlfriend Babs Doniger, 'You keep asking me how I crossed the ocean – I can't say but it should be pretty obvious – one reason you didn't hear from me for so long. I wasn't sick.' However, most were much more open, like **Paul Steichen** (93 BG):

So far the trip has been perfect. We are in a convoy so there is little to worry about. It is cool and the sea is calm and not a soul seasick. We came aboard expecting the worst but found very good conditions. Searles, Pete, Glauner and I are sharing a stateroom with six others. I've been catching up on sleep most of the day. They have a very good officers' mess, tablecloths, choice of menu and waiters thrown in. Had half a grapefruit, All Bran, bacon, eggs, coffee for breakfast with roast beef full course dinner tonight.

Not all the men were good sailors. **John van Acker** (491 BG):

About the third day out almost everyone lost his breakfast (including me). I didn't feel so well after going below to see my crew. The rail was visited quite a few times and those on the lower decks had to watch out because swarms of men were testing out the rail – of course there were those who didn't make it. Anyway most people got over being seasick ... We wonder if it will be possible to walk straight again when we get on firm ground. It will also be quite dull to sit down to a dinner table again and not have your chair slip and tip out from under you; also to see all the plates of food, cups and bowls stand still will be a novelty after this trip!

**John Rex**, Military Policeman: 'My bunk on this crossing was on the open starboard lifeboat deck, we slept on that deck. The redeeming feature of this location was that the lifeboats were only a few feet away.'

The voyage over (John van Acker).

A good many men crossed on board the *Queen Mary*, as did **Willis Wood Marshall** (389 BG):

> We were at Kilmer about two weeks before being taken to New York and put aboard the *Queen Mary*. We spent several days on board while that great liner filled with some 24/25,000 troops of all types. They had put an auxiliary floor in a main dining room. We were on the upper part of the auxiliary floor near the top of the *Queen* and the aft part of this great ship. Finally on November third, we departed New York, headed down the Hudson River and out into the Atlantic. Most of us who were able to, watched the Statue of Liberty for as long as we could see it … One thing that always stuck with me was that Ken was the only pilot of the ten that came to check on how the enlisted men were faring. I think Ken made that visit every day and always brought peanut butter crackers, candy bars etc.

**Harold Both** (492 BG):

To our American palates the food was horrible on board the *Queen*, but, for breakfast I managed to make do with oatmeal because my parents were Norwegians and as a result I was well broken into oatmeal for breakfast instead of kippers.

**Kenneth D. Jones** (389 BG) was one of 15,000 men on board the *Queen Mary*:

Fresh water for drinking was limited to one canteen full a day. Washing and shaving was done with salt water and a special soap called 'sand soap'. Ordinary soap would not lather in salt water. I shaved only once. The pain of shaving wasn't worth the effort. There were no facilities for a bath or shower so we were pretty gamey by the time we got to England (the voyage took six days).

Others travelled by 'liberty ship', in which they had less confidence. **Frederick R. Porter** (467 BG) recalled:

During the crossing on the *USATS Frederick Lykes*, I was 'fortunate' enough to pull the deck watch detail. The main duty was to ensure that there was no smoking on deck. The light from a burning cigarette would make us a target for German U-Boats. The advantage of this assignment was that it gave an excuse to get away from the stench of the passenger hold … The *Lykes* was a liberty ship which apparently had been built on an assembly line. In civilian life I had been an engineer in a metal fabricating shop so I knew what reliable welds were supposed to look like. The *Lykes* looked like it had been welded by amateurs so I was very relieved when we made it all the way across the Atlantic with the ship still intact.

**Joseph L. Nathan** (448 BG):

Left New York aboard the *USS General Black* headed for England. It was a liberty ship and not too comfortable, although we officers were far better off than the poor enlisted men who were packed in like sardines in hot holds.

Some men were in transit on Thanksgiving Day, but it was not a special occasion. **John van Acker**: 'In your letter you spoke of Thanksgiving dinner, but I guess I already wrote about our Thanksgiving on the boat. A fancy menu with message signed by FDR but no food to match.'

Women in the WACs (described later), also came over by ship. **Mary Frances Williams** (who became Elder on her marriage in 1946):

*On the boat*: Dearest Family: Are you very surprised? I know you are, and worried too, but please don't be. You remember when I wrote about the First Separate Battalion, how good it was, and that we were a specially picked group – Well, now you know how true it was. We are good and we are special. Believe me, if you could see me now, sitting in the top side of a double decker swaying with the movement of the boat. I'm really beginning to walk like a sailor – One of the girls watched me coming down the corridor and said I was walking at a 45 degree angle. It will take some time to get my land legs again.

Haven't been sea sick a bit. One of the girls I'm bunking with, the one in the lower half of the bed, was sick the first day out. Cohen – you remember I wrote you about her – Oh she was sick – but has fully recovered now. In fact, was playing skip-rope on deck this afternoon. The weather has been beautiful up to the last day or so, but even raining it's still a treat to go on deck and watch the water. I didn't know the water could be such a heavenly blue and turn so suddenly into steel gray. Now I know why Bill Rader joined the Navy. I can see the call of the sea in the faces of the men who run the ship. They call 'her' – 'she' – 'the old lady' and any other endearing terms that would fit a lady.

They were greater dangers than sea sickness: German submarines were lying in wait. **Willis Marshall:**

On our voyage over somewhere off the northwest coast of France they picked up a submarine wolf pack lying in wait for the *Queen Mary*. The *Mary* could outrun a sub so the captain went to full speed and started zig zagging. There was very heavy seas and along with the zig zagging made for a very rough night. I can remember lying on the very narrow bunk and rolling from side to side. I know I didn't get much sleep and I don't think the other troops did either. I can remember hearing aircraft that arrived on the scene around 11 p.m. They were around for a couple of hours. The next morning when we went on deck there were two Canadian destroyer escorts on each side preceding us towards the Irish seas. The waves were so high that those DEs [destroyer escorts] would completely disappear from our view and we were on the very top deck of the *Mary*. On November ninth we arrived in the Firth of Clyde and debarked on what they called lighters to the docks at Gourick [*sic* - Gourock], Scotland.

**James Caulfield** (492 BG) remembered, 'We left the States on the 24th March 1943 in a convoy from New York to Liverpool. We were sixteen days crossing in a small ship called the *Jean* and almost did not make it as we lost thirteen ships all around us.'

# Chapter Two

# First Impressions

The very first impressions on reaching England varied enormously.
  **Mary Williams-Elder**, 19 July 1943:

> The first night we got here we had French fried potatoes and pork chops. What a reception. Since then we've had the best food I've had since I left home. For instance, yesterday we had meat loaf, sweet potatoes candied, cabbage slaw, raisin bread – gravy, canned peaches and coffee for lunch. For dinner we had pork roast and believe me it was good. I've never eaten such food, in all the time I've been in the Army.

**John van Acker:**

> The countryside looks so peaceful with its quaint old houses etc. Only the ears can detect the fact that a war is on. On the whole the country here looks very neat. Everything is very old looking and well established. The people are pretty shabbily clothed but they all look pretty rugged. They have to be to live in this climate because it sure is cold… All I can tell you is that our base is not very fancy. We might just as well be in the mud of France or the cold of Ireland. There is one very small stove in each barracks, smaller than a kerosene stove, and we can't keep it going all the time.

**Alfred Neumunz** to Babs: 'To answer your question on my likes and dislikes of this country it is mostly a dislike. Although a rather pretty place it is very dirty – which is probably due to the long years at war. Then also I'm still in the army which isn't a place of my liking.'
  The official *Handbook* issued to American troops warned them about the British weather:

> If you are from Boston or Seattle the weather may remind you of home. If you are from Arizona or North Dakota you will find it a little hard to get used to. At first you will probably not like the almost continual rains and mists and the absence of crisp cold. Actually, the city of London has less rain for the whole year than many places in the United States, but the rain falls in frequent drizzles. Most people get used to the English climate eventually.

Many of the newcomers were used to a much warmer and drier climate, and there were many comments on the weather in England, almost all unfavourable.

**Rudolph Howell** (389 BG):

I hate English weather. When we first got here we had about three days of beautiful weather – nearly perfect. Then it got sloppy again and they say most of the time it is sloppy. I hate it. It is the most depressing thing you could think of. The air is about 50% water and it's like living in a damp dungeon. The sun is generally obscured and it is the dreariest thing imaginable.

**Charles Barlow** (448 BG) was from California, arriving in October 1943: 'I am in England. It is a very pretty country. The weather is going to be very hard to get used to. It is very damp and you seldom see the sun. The climate is supposed to be about like Seattle Washington.'

**Clayton C. Wiseman** (392 BG), 20 March 1944: 'One of those damn English days, cold and wet.'

**Paul Steichen**: 'What miserable weather this is. I can't get warm in bed, 4 blankets and all.' Five days later he wrote: 'Tonight I'm going to put all my overcoats etc. over me before I get in the sack.'

**Curtis Anderson** was also depressed at first, writing:

25 Oct 1944: When we get through I hope never to see England again. I wouldn't live here if they gave me this damned island. Weather, oh well!

29 Oct: getting colder and nastier, if possible.

2 Nov: rain and more of it. Getting colder too. Snow would be the last straw.

**John van Acker**: 'I hope that you didn't get any pajamas because I have found that it is too cold to change. The best thing to do is to sleep in long underwear.'

**Rudolph Howell**, 29 April 1945:

The weather is really remarkable. A couple of weeks ago we were having some of the nicest spring weather anyone could ask for. It almost turned into summer. A lot of fellows were out taking sun baths. Then it turned a bit colder and we started having that cloudy, dreary, rainy weather again. And yesterday morning I woke up and saw the straw that broke the camel's back when I looked out of the window and saw that it was snowing. There it was the 28th of April and we were having a snow storm.

In a later letter, he wrote

Well, I haven't complained about the weather so long I guess I'm getting used to it. Yesterday I saw the sun for the first time in over a week, if I remember correctly. The fellow across the hall wrote his wife that they hadn't yet decided whether summer was going to be a half a day or a whole day this year.

The English weather: Nissen huts under snow at Rackheath.

The complications of the English system of money also caused some difficulties at first.

**Mary Williams-Elder**, 19 July 1943:

Are we having a time with the English money. I wonder who in the world ever thought up such a complicated system. It is rather hard to get accustomed to thinking in pence, shillings, half-crowns, crowns, pounds etc. But the boys say that after a while you get so you don't even think of American money. You should see the pennies. They are as large as a half-dollar, only they are copper. The half-crown is also the size of a half-dollar but it is silver, you have to look to see which is which.

**Rudolph Howell:**

Getting used to this new money is quite a job, what with some things costing four shillings six and a hapence, and others costing two pounds three or something like that. They told us that an English penny was worth two cents American and that three English pennies (thripence) were worth 5 cents American, so everyone consequently got confused. I was about the first to emerge from the fog, so Parsons and Deleot began asking me how much change that they should get if they gave the fellow that blue note and things like that. One day they ran across a problem that stumped everyone. They gave someone £1 (one pound) and he changed it into a ten shilling note, three half crowns, a florin and a sixpence, and nobody could figure out if he had been gyped. So I walked up and calmly explained the whole British monetary system and convinced them that they hadn't been gyped.

The *Handbook* prepared the incomers on all aspects of life in Britain:

Remember there's a war on. Britain may look a little shop-worn and grimy to you. The British people are anxious to have you know that you are not seeing their country at its best. There's been a war on since 1939. The houses haven't been painted because factories are not making paint – they're making planes. The famous English gardens and parks are either unkept because there are no men to take care of them, or they are being used to grow needed vegetables. British taxicabs look antique because Britain makes tanks for herself and Russia and hasn't time to make new cars. British trains are cold because power is needed for industry, not for heating. There are no luxury dining cars on trains because total work effort has no place for such frills. The trains are unwashed and grimy because men and women are needed for more important work than car-washing. The British people are anxious for you to know that in normal times Britain looks much prettier, cleaner, neater… You came to Britain from a country where your home is still safe, food is still plentiful, and lights are still burning. So it is doubly important for you to remember that the British soldiers and civilians are living under a tremendous strain. It is always impolite to criticize your hosts. It is militarily stupid to insult your allies. So stop and think before you sound off about lukewarm beer, or cold boiled potatoes, or the way English cigarettes taste.

If British people look dowdy and badly dressed, it is not because they do not like good clothes or know how to wear them. All clothing is rationed and the British know that they help war production by wearing an old suit or dress until it cannot be patched any longer. Old clothes are 'good form'.

One thing to be careful about – if you are invited into a British home and the host exhorts you to 'eat up – there's plenty on the table', go easy. It may be the family's rations for a whole week spread out to show their hospitality.

**Some Important Dos And Don'ts:**

*Be Friendly* – but don't intrude anywhere it seems you are not wanted.

You will find the British money system easier than you think. A little study beforehand on shipboard will make it still easier.

You are higher paid than the British 'Tommy'. Don't rub it in. Play fair with him. He can be a pal in need.

Don't show off or brag or bluster – 'swank' as the British say. If somebody looks in your direction and says, 'He's chucking his weight about,' you can be pretty sure you're off base. That's the time to pull in your ears.

If you are invited to eat with a family don't eat too much. Otherwise you may eat up their weekly rations.

Don't make fun of British speech or accents. You sound just as funny to them but they will be too polite to show it.

Avoid comments on the British Government or politics.

Don't try to tell the British that America won the last war or make wisecracks about the war debts or about British defeats in this war.

*Never* criticize the King or Queen.

Don't criticize the food, beer, or cigarettes to the British. Remember they have been at war since 1939.

Use common sense on all occasions. By your conduct you have great power to bring about a better understanding between the two countries after the war is over.

You will soon find yourself among a kindly, quiet, hard-working people who have been living under a strain such as few people in the world have ever known. In your dealings with them, let this be your slogan: *It is always impolite to criticize your hosts; it is militarily stupid to criticize your allies.*

Language was going to be a problem too. The *Handbook* offered up an explanation of some of the words an American might find strange in Britain. Equally, the British would find some words the Americans used rather bizarre.

From *Glossary of Terms*:

| American | English |
|---|---|
| ale | beer OR bitter |
| ash can | dustbin |
| automobile | motor car OR car |
| baggage car | luggage van |
| bartender | barman OR potman |
| beer | lager |
| bouncer | chucker out |
| candy (hard) | boiled sweets |
| candy store | sweet shop |
| cookie | biscuit |
| dessert | sweet |
| drawers (men's) | pants |
| druggist | chemist |
| drug store | chemist's shop |
| drygoods store | draper's shop |
| elevator | lift |
| five-and-ten (store) | bazaar |
| fresh fruit | dessert (at the end of a meal) |
| french fried potatoes | chips |
| gear shift | gear lever |
| hardware | ironmongery |
| highball | whiskey and soda |
| hunting | shooting |

| | |
|---|---|
| instalment plan | hire purchase system |
| janitor | caretaker OR porter |
| junk | rubbish |
| living room | sitting room |
| long distance (telephone) | trunks |
| marriage certificate | marriage lines |
| movie house | cinema |
| movies | flicks |
| mucilage | gum |
| pitcher | jug |
| potato chips | crisps |

The *Handbook* also explained the thinking behind the censorship of soldiers' letters:

*Think!* Where does the enemy get his information – information that can put you, and has put your comrades, adrift on an open sea; information that has lost battles and can lose more, unless you personally, vigilantly perform your duty in safeguarding military information?

*Censorship rules are simple, sensible.* – They are merely concise statements drawn from actual experience briefly outlining the types of material which have proved to be disastrous when available to the enemy. A soldier should not hesitate to impose his own additional rules when he is considering writing of a subject not covered

*Above and next page:* Initial impressions – the weather and the language! (Jack Preston).

by present regulations. He also should be on guard against false rumours and misstatements about censorship. It is sometimes stated that censorship delays mail for long periods of time. Actually all mail (with certain nominal and very unusual exceptions) is completely through censorship within 48 hours.

**There are ten prohibited subjects:**

1. Don't write military information of Army units – their location, strength, material, or equipment.
2. Don't write of military installations.
3. Don't write of transportation facilities.
4. Don't write of convoys, their routes, ports (including ports of embarkation and disembarkation), time en route, naval protection, or war incidents occurring en route.
5. Don't disclose movements of ships, naval or merchant, troops, or aircraft.
6. Don't mention plans and forecasts or orders for future operations, whether known or just your guess.
7. Don't write about the effects of enemy operations.
8. Don't tell of any casualty until released by proper authority (The Adjutant General) and then only by using the full name of the casualty.
9. Don't attempt to formulate or use a code system, cipher, or shorthand, or any other means to conceal the true meaning of your letter. Violations of this regulation will result in severe punishment.
10. Don't give your location in any way except as authorized by proper authority. Be sure nothing you write about discloses a more specific location than the one authorized.

**When You Are Overseas**

*V-Mail*: this is an expeditious mail program which provides for quick mail service to and from soldiers overseas. A special form is used which permits the letter to be photographed on microfilm, the small film transported, and then reproduced and delivered. Use of *V-Mail* is urged because it greatly furthers the war effort by saving shipping and airplane space.

**Rudolph Howell** soon came up against the language issue:

The British use lots of words different from us. I haven't been among them enough to know many of the words, but I have picked up some of them. I saw some advertisements for 'twin prams' (baby carriages), and automobile 'tyres'. A sign pointed to 'Ladies' Lavatories'. At sandwich stands the 'tarriff' is three pence per 'bisquit'. You don't line up to eat, you queue up. I think 'bloody' is about the worst word in their vocabulary and 'fanny' is unspeakable [To an American, it merely meant 'bottom'].

He soon noticed other oddities: 'British trains are really the stuff. They travel at about 10½ mph or something like that, and just about as comfortable as a box car.'

In a later letter, he revised his opinion:

> The typical train that you see in the movies with compartments and everything. It really travelled fast, and it started and stopped so smoothly that you actually couldn't tell if you were moving without looking out the window. The engines are so small they don't look like they will pull a train. And the doggone goods wagons (freight cars to you) are so little and dinky you could put two of them in one of ours, and have room to spare. They only have four wheels and the wheels have spokes. They aren't solid like ours. Nothing over here is big like it is back home. That was one of the first things that struck me after I got here. There's just a certain feeling you get when you see the difference. Back home everything was just taken for granted, but things back there are just big.

**Mary Williams-Elder** was another sharp observer:

> Of course we have been looking the country over and have discovered some very interesting sights. In a little town over here, for instance, they have, instead of having 'No Parking' signs on one side of the street, they have signs saying to park on one side of the street on even days and the other side on odd days. Now doesn't that sound funny. Another thing is the warm beer they have. Of course that doesn't bother me, but some of the other girls have tried it, and they don't like it very much, but I guess they will get used to it in time.

**John Rex** also recorded his first impressions:

> After arriving in England several things struck me as quite depressing. At night there was a strict blackout, no lights anywhere, and this was quite often coupled with the fog or heavy mist. It was like trying to find your way around in a coal mine without any lights. The second thing that struck me was the lack of modern plumbing as we knew it here in Audubon. Thirdly, the physical condition of much of the property, in so many cases in a state of disrepair. Building supplies for civilians were non existent and so was the labour to use it. We quickly learned of all the shortages the civilians had to endure. Remember, by this time they had been in a war for four years. Eggs were severely rationed to them and were non existent in our diet also, fresh eggs that is. We found our way around that, we traded with the local farmers: sugar for eggs.

The overall reaction from local people was one of support: after two or more years of fighting Germany alone, a powerful ally was here to help. **Charles Barlow** summed it up: 'The people here are very friendly and glad to see American soldiers.'

## Chapter Three

# The Pilots and Crew

The greatest number of letters and memoirs are from the men who actually flew in the planes. The pilots of course spent many months training in the States before crossing the channel.

**Robert Boyle:**

Fort Worth, Texas, 28 March 1943: today was the day. I had my first airplane ride this morning, and was it swell. The weather cleared up Friday evening, and yesterday the ground dried out enough for us to use the field today. It was a funny thing, though, when you are up, you have no sense of forward motion at all. You could be going 40 mph or 400 mph, and you still think you are standing still. If you can imagine a plane suspended on a wire, and it just assumes different positions in relation to the earth, you have some idea of what it is like. I was up for 47 minutes, and for about one third of that time I actually flew the plane. Just getting the feel of it, and getting on to the idea of using your hands and feet at the same time. No kidding, it's fun.

Just three days later, he wrote:

I've been flying every day this week, and it sure is swell. You'd be surprised though, how tired you get after flying for an hour. I guess I'm making out as good as the rest of the fellows, but there sure is a heck of a lot to remember all at once. You don't have time to think. Yesterday, we practiced spins. That was some thrill, and I don't mean maybe.

**Willis Marshall:**

While at St Xavier we received ten hours of flight training. This consisted of pre-flight – take-off manoeuvres and landings. The sixth hour another inspector flew with us to inspect our programs. When my sixth hour came, I had a lady inspector. We taxied out to the end of the runway, checked the engine and the sky for any other planes. The inspector said OK, let's do it. I shoved the throttle forward and turned onto the runway, a grass strip. With this I think, I held the left rudder pedal and we spun around in a circle. In essence we ground looped. The inspector chopped the throttle or we might have been still spinning. She said let's not do that again, it didn't feel so good. So I proceeded to recheck the engine and sky and entered onto the runway again. Needless to say I was so nervous that my check ride didn't go so well. I did get through the ten hours of flight training and still wanted to be a pilot.

**Ken Jones:**

The highly sought wings were won and commission granted at Lubbock, Texas in April, 1944. Those of us who selected multi-engined aircraft were assigned to B-24s at Liberal, Kansas after graduation from advanced flight school. The B-24 had a bad reputation in the training command. There were a lot of accidents. No one was happy to get this assignment. We all wanted the 'glory wagon' the B-17 Flying Fortress.

As we became more familiar with the airplane, we started giving the B-24 raunchy names of affection. The 'Truck', the 'Whistling Outhouse', the 'Firetrap' etc. The B-24 was ugly but beautiful and a joy forever.

There was more training at the airbases in Britain.
  **Ed Scamahorn** (491 BG):

19 Aug: the crew and I were in school all day today learning about the Darky system of navigation, occult and Pundit lights, searchlight aids and the many various Q signals for radio work.

B-24 'Alfred II' at Wendling in the snow

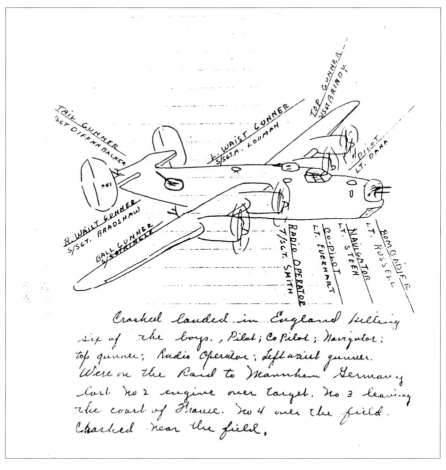

Diagram to show typical lay-out of pilots and crew on a B-24

22 Aug: learned the call signs of the different squadrons. Each squadron flies about ten bombers on a mission and a group mission will normally have 30 planes. This leaves one squadron in reserve for rest and repair.

23 Aug: Today we went on a short local formation flight. I flew with another pilot acting as co-pilot. He has ten missions to his credit and was to show me how to fly formation here. The trip was uneventful and we landed just in time for supper. I wonder why I am always so hungry?

24 Aug: We flew again today. This time we flew as a crew, no strangers on board. We were briefed on the weather and formation procedure. We took off on runway 24 and went on instruments at 3,000 ft. Freezing level was at 11,000 and we began to ice up. We used the de-icers and continued on up. We finally broke out at 23,000 ft, and were still not on top of all the cloud cover. There was about a quarter of an inch of snow in the navigator's compartment. We managed to find the rest of the formation and flew a practise mission at 25,000. Coming home we let down over the North Sea and came over the coast at about 400 ft. It was raining hard at the field and foggy. We would never have found the place if they hadn't been firing yellow-yellow flares at the approach end of the runway. There must be an easier way to make a living.

After the training, it was time for the first mission. This was a moment that men remembered all their lives.

**J. Ray Bickel** (467 BG):

They issued the rest of our flying gear such as Mae Wests [inflatable life vests], parachutes, steel helmets, goggles, throat mikes, and black, high top civilian shoes. The throat mikes were held to our throat by an elastic band. Each unit had two small microphones that fit against the sides of our throat, one each side of our 'Adam's Apple'.

The radio system in the planes had feedback so we could hear how our own voice sounded. That way we could learn how to speak so that the others would understand us. The mike cord had a switch that we could depress when we wanted to talk. The pilots' mike buttons were fastened to a spoke on the control wheel. This way we all had our hands free to do other things. The black shoes were to be carried each time we were over enemy territory. They were tied together with parachute shroud lines and fastened to the parachute harness with a metal snap in case we had to bail out. Those shoes had two purposes. One was that the flying boots were not suitable for walking. The other was that if we got down safely and undetected, we were less apt to be spotted in black civilian shoes than in brown army issue shoes. They also gave us a large canvas bag, called a parachute bag, to carry the gear out to the plane in. The briefing hut was an extra large Nissen hut where crews met before each mission to get instructions for the mission. It was also the place where everyone came back to at the end of the mission to change clothes and be debriefed.

We were awakened about 2 a.m., got dressed, showered (electric Remington) went to the latrine, and on to a breakfast of powdered eggs, toast, and coffee. Then on to briefing where the target, course, turning points etc were marked on a huge map with heavy yarn connecting the points enroute. After the general briefing we had a separate

Getting ready for take off

briefing by Major Holmes. The navigators were given the times, course turning points, altitude wind direction and speed, target and alternate target information and the location of anti-aircraft batteries enroute and in the target area.

When the briefings were over, we went to the locker room to finish dressing. We put our electric flying suits over our uniforms, then the heavy B-13 jacket, leather helmet and flying boots. We also had the parachute pack, the black shoes, parachute harness, the Mae West and the steel helmet all placed in a large canvas bag to be taken to the plane.

The first plane to take off was an old B-24D painted with colored circles. This was the formation ship ... The planes took off at 30 second intervals and started to circle over nondirectional radio beacons called splashers and bunchers that the British had set up to be used as navigation aids. It usually took about two hours from the time the planes started to take off until the lead plane departed the English coast.

When the time to depart arrived, the lead Group flew over the departure point. Other wings and groups fell into a trail formation called a bomber stream made up of more than 2000 B-24's and B-17's.

## Ken Jones:

We are placed on alert on Dec 1st. A letter is written home, all personal identification removed from clothing, .45 ammo loaded in clips for pistol and knife placed in flying boot. We talk a little bit about tomorrow and then are silent as each one deals with his own private thoughts. Sleep doesn't come. Finally, dozing in the early morning, someone makes the rounds, waking up the mission crews for 04.00 hours. Breakfast included powdered eggs and powdered milk. Tasteless food. Didn't eat much.

At the general briefing, the black curtain on stage was opened and we saw our penetration route into Germany and learned the location of the target for the first time … A huge map of Europe with a red tape extending from base in England to the target and back. There were red blotches of transparent overlays indicating flak concentrations and menacing looking German fighter planes in tiny silhouettes. There were some audible groans …

The mission is on. The big birds begin to move out of the parking areas. Slowly leaving the hardstands in precise order, to the perimeter taxi strip. A picture of big, slab sided geese full of feed heading for the pond and an early morning swim. Bill to tail – waddling to the end of the runway rolling and dipping along – squeeking [sic] brakes.

Our turn to jump off the cliff. We run up the engines on the final check list and swing out to point down the take-off runway … Cowl flaps closing. We get the green light from the tower … releasing brakes, full throttle and rolling. Gear up we plunged into the overcast [cloud]. We broke into the clear at about 8,000 ft, on top of the overcast. Still climbing to formation altitude of 10,000 ft. Heading for Buncher 6 and we spot the red–green flares which separates our group from the hundreds of bombers nosing through the blue in the distance. It went like clockwork. We eased into our formation position in the slot, off our element leader.

**Phillip G. Day** (467 BG):

I flew my first mission in olive drab wool shirt and trousers. I wasn't superstitious (much) but I continued wearing this shirt and trousers on all of my other combat missions. I wore a tee shirt and boxer shorts under these. Over the ODs, I would wear a flying suit that was heated electrically from the plane's electrical system, the amount of heat controlled by a rheostat. On my feet I wore a pair of heavy wool RAF issue socks and over these electrically heated boots connected to the suit. Over these I wore fleece-lined rubber-soled, zippered flying boots. Over the electrical flying suit I wore a padded pair of pants with a high waist supported by suspenders and a padded jacket with mouton collar, later a hooded jacket. On my hands I wore an inner pair of silk gloves and over these fleece lined gloves with cuffs up over the jacket cuffs. We wore a life vest, bright orange yellow, inflated by pulling a lanyard that released a $CO_2$ cartridge or that could be inflated by mouth through a tube. I wore a back pack type parachute, its harness over the 'Mae West' life vest. On reaching 12,000 feet we put on our oxygen masks which attached to our flying helmets. We wore eye protection consisting of a goggle type holder with changeable lens, generally using green because of sun glare. We had throat mikes which were like two large buttons held against your throat with an elastic band. Around my neck I wore a parachute silk scarf. Prior to entering enemy controlled territory we put on a steel helmet that covered down to the upper neck area and had flaps over the ears. And over all the clothing, life vest, a parachute and harness we wore a flak suit consisting of steel pieces sewn into a canvas material that was apron like in front, from the lower back over the shoulders, down the front and ending in the crotch area and having closures to the sides. We were quite comfortable as to warmth when the electric suits worked properly and not too uncomfortable if they malfunctioned … All others of the crew wore similar clothing and gear, except that their parachutes were chest packs, detached and carried separately, that had to be snapped onto the harness if needed.

People that get on to a passenger plane today have no conception of what it was like to fly in an unpressurised plane like the B-24. It was open to the elements, so once you were many thousands of feet up the atmosphere was extremely cold and there simply was not enough oxygen in the air for a man to breathe. This could easily kill. There are many stories of crew suffering because of a failure in their oxygen supply.

**Gerald Edwards** (492 BG) recalled how his Texas training lecture had saved his life on a mission:

This man was talking about oxygen. He was telling us what it was like if your oxygen was leaking or if you didn't have any. He said that everything would become really peaceful and nice, real warm. You just floated on cloud nine if your oxygen goes out. On one of my missions, I can't remember which one. Man, it was always so cold up there, I got so warm, so peaceful and everything was just heavenly. That came to me in my mind what the man had said. I looked down and my oxygen hose had become unhooked! I barely had enough strength to snap it together again. I got it back together and boy was I miserable. I was cold and shivering, sweating but if I had missed that training lecture that day I would have just kept on going and that would be it.

**Burt Frauman** (458 BG), flying from Horsham in December 1944, began to feel light-headed:

I gasped in horror as the terror of the potential consequences engulfed me – Anoxia! I fought the panic as my mind flashed back to the 'guinea pig' experience in the chamber at Selman Field. How long would I retain rational behaviour, or before I passed out? Think! My mask had been working fine; I had been getting an adequate supply.

I traced back from the mask to the oxygen tank for signs of a break or rupture. Then I checked the flexible tubing that was firm and solid instead of soft. Apparently the bitter cold, coupled with long periods of being static while trying to warm my hands, had allowed my breath moisture to freeze and build up as ice, so restricting the oxygen flow…This was the likely explanation since this situation had not occurred before.

I began crushing the tubing, which brought no result for a few anxious moments, but as I squeezed harder I could hear the ice breaking up. 'Thank God it is not yet solid with ice, there is a core of air' was my thought. I turned the oxygen tank control to 100% and inhaled deeply while extremely conscious of my mental state – or lack of it. I cautioned myself to turn the control back to normal, otherwise I would run down the supply.

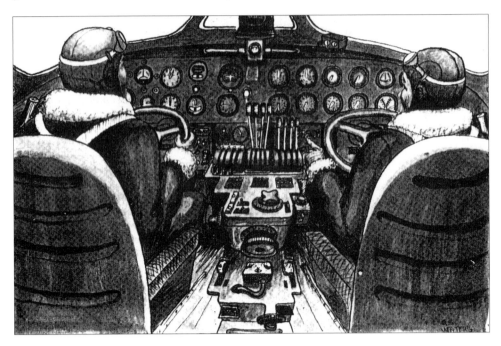

Inside a B-24 (Ray Waters).

One of the crew had already passed out, but Frauman was able to revive him, and radio silence was broken to let other crew know the situation and make their own checks.

The flights had to be aborted if there was no oxygen, as in an instance recorded by **James McCrery** (492 BG) on 11 July 1944: '15.25 hours. Leak in oxygen supply - approximately half of our oxygen supply was gone in our first hour at altitude, with oxygen needed for five hours more. Flew to enemy coast with oxygen supply decreasing rapidly, turned around and returned to base.'

Because the flights might easily last six or eight hours, there were other problems involving man's most basic functions: eating and relieving oneself.

**Robert Doyle:**

Virginia wonders how I can eat with that oxygen mask on. Well, we just take it off for a moment, and eat if we want to. Sometimes we smoke, but it's almost impossible to strike a match at 4 or 5 miles up. After all, if there was no air at all, you could hold your breath for 30 seconds at least, we have some air so we can go longer than that. Simple isn't it?

**Ken Jones:**

Another rather urgent altitude problem in the confines of limited aircraft space was answering a call of nature in the sub-zero temperatures of rarefied atmosphere ... The relief tube was located in the bomb bay. It was necessary to disconnect your oxygen hose from the ship's main system, take a 'walk around' oxygen bottle, struggle back to a crowded bomb bay, dig through layers of clothing and an electric flying suit. You 'hurried right along' to avoid frostbite. Then as you returned to your combat position, you continuously snagged your oxygen hose, mike cord, electric suit cord and heavy clothing on every bulkhead and other protrusions. If flak started or you came under fighter attack during the process of attending to the call of nature, a mild panic set in and it became real exciting.

Missions of course varied enormously in character. Sometimes they would not be completed due to changes in the weather. These might be regarded as sorties rather than missions and would not count towards the total number of missions. Completed missions might face no opposition at all – these were nicknamed 'milk runs'. Other missions might face overwhelming opposition from enemy planes or anti-aircraft guns – or both. Most of the airmen kept track of their missions by drawing a bomb onto their leather jackets. At Old Buckenham a refinement of this was to draw a bomb for a tough mission, a milk bottle for a milk run!

Flak and enemy fighters were the two dangers that had to be faced on most missions, and there are many descriptions of their effect. **J. Ray Bickel**: 'Flak was an abbreviation of a number of German words describing their anti-aircraft artillery, *Flieger Abwehr Kanonen*.' On a mission to Hamburg, he recorded:

What an awful lot of flak. The most flak I ever saw or ever want to see. I was watching the bombs go away and couldn't see where they were landing so I stuck my head out the side window. Thirty seconds later a piece of flak spattered the glass below the bombsight into a million pieces. Some of which flew up to the pilot's flight deck. My desk was covered with glass from a hole three inches long and one inch wide. I only found a piece of flak about one inch by one inch. The flak is a jagged piece of cheap steel.

Nose Art: Flak Magnet II

**Curtis Anderson,** 14 October 1944: 'Flak intense, but not any hits until we got to the lines. Then Simpson got a slug clear through his left leg. So cold blood froze as it came out.'

**Vyto J. Enovitch** (448 BG):

Crossed enemy coast at 11:15. That's where fun began. We must have been off course, cause at about Coblenz the enemy began shelling us with flak. Oh, my goodness, I never was so scared in all my youthful days. The sky was just filled with puffs of black smoke which consequently sprayed us with shrapnel. I thought we'd never get out of it … the sky was just one solid mass of black puffs and about 500 B-24's right in the center of it.

The effects of flak can be seen in the story of **Leon Vance.** As his Liberator started on its bomb run over coastal France, it was subjected to a continuous hail of heavy flak and suffered repeated hits. The bombardier, Milton Segal, was not wearing his flak helmet when the first burst hit the nose of the ship. He left his bombsight for a second to get it, and then returned to his position. As he bent over his sight a second burst caught the nose knocking Segal's helmet from his head. This time he did not attempt to retrieve it. Over the interphone he informed Louis Mazure, the pilot, that he would take control for the final run. 'I've got the ship', he said.

'Good boy', replied the pilot.

Those were his last words, for a piece of flak struck him in the temple immediately afterwards and killed him instantly. With the pilot dead the Liberator continued over the target and bombs were released.

Meanwhile the entire ship was in an uproar. 'At approximately the same time as the pilot was killed, the command pilot received a hit that blew off his left foot above the ankle'. The navigator, Bernard Bail, applied a tourniquet that saved his life. Meanwhile the co-pilot had taken control as the pilot slumped over the controls and after hearing the words 'Bombs Away', swung the nose of the ship toward England. 'At this point the command pilot who had managed to pull himself to his feet braced himself between the pilots' seats and leaned over and pulled the throttle, then pushed it back. 'No Power,' he told Earl Carper, the co-pilot, 'Cut all switches.' This Carper did and they began the glide back to the British coast.

'We dropped 5,000 feet in what seemed like a second', related Carper. 'A B-24 isn't much of a glider but we got back over England. The colonel was the bravest guy I ever saw,' he continued, 'When we got over land he told all the crew to bail out and then wanted me to try and ditch it'. Carper, who had watched the ship lose more and more altitude, wanted the command pilot to bail out, but he refused and told Carper to leave. The co-pilot jumped over land but, as they had turned the nose again after the rest of the crew had bailed out, he landed in the Channel. The command pilot sat on the edge of the seat and refused to leave the ship. He pulled back the controls, which was all that could be done to ditch the ship. The Liberator landed and he was flown clear. In a test of physical stamina that defies explanation, the one-legged man swam for three miles in the icy water before he was picked up by a rescue ship.

"B-24"

A B-24 in flight (Ray Waters).

Vance was given America's highest military award, the Medal of Honor. He died when the evacuation aircraft on which he was being taken back to America was lost without trace over the Atlantic.

Some airmen feared attack from German planes at least as much as flak.

**Joseph Nathan**, 25 March 1945:

I have never seen a German fighter on a mission, but I fear them more than flak. Flak is impersonal. It's aimed at you as lead ship, but it hits in the squadron. Fighters are different. They single out a ship, often the lead, and bear down on him. Today they clung to Stalland from the IP to the target: that's a hell of a lot different from a flak burst. Mixed feelings – the age old question, 'Why Stalland?' – a twinge of fear – a hatred for the Germans who are killing for a lost cause, bringing others down with them as they sink.

The planes flew in daylight, many hundreds of bombers flying in strict formation to their targets. The sight of such aerial power made an unforgettable impression on Norfolk people, many of whom counted out the planes and then counted them as they came back, hoping that there were no losses among their new allies. With so many planes flying in formation, there was always a risk of error, leading to crashes or to episodes of 'friendly fire'. These could well involve the deaths of all those involved.

**Willis Marshall** was a witness to one:

A mission was scheduled to bomb Bordeaux, France. A force of Germans was holding out and the Allies had them surrounded. This was just a small force that was holed up there ... A bombing mission was set up and I was told that originally we were scheduled to fly on the 14th [April 1945]. For one reason or another we were taken off that list and another crew put on the list. The 24s happened to be on the same target that the 17s were with the 17s at a higher altitude. They dropped their deadly cargo right on the hapless B24s knocking six of them down. I believe the 24s were three minutes early and the 17s were 17 minutes late which put them there at the same time.

One of the worst accidents occurred on 29 March 1944. Two B-24s based at Hardwick crashed into each other over Henham Park in Suffolk. They were returning from a bombing mission against the U-Boat pens in Normandy. Seventeen of the twenty airmen on board the two planes were killed, and the tragedy was compounded when an explosion in the wreckage killed another nineteen people engaged in rescue work.

Extracts from the diary of **Richard N. Vincent** (445 BG) record his first six missions:

March 17 [1945]: Today is the day we have long awaited. Our target was Munster Germany and as the old timers say 'It was a milk run'. We dropped 44 one hundred pound bombs and 2 one hundred pound incendiary clusters on the marshalling yards. Our squadron was lucky as we encountered no flak, but other squadrons were not so lucky. We bombed through 10/10 clouds by PFF (Radar) and the results were good. Matt was a little excited and we nearly got a P-51 which was mistook for a 262 Jet Job.

March 22: Everything went wrong today and our plane was forced to abandon the mission out over the North Sea as we were about to enter Holland. John [the navigator] accidentally hit the salvo switch and jettisoned our bombs along with the bomb doors.

March 23: Rough – and rough is putting it mildly. I hope I never have another mission like that. We went to Munster again only this time there were no clouds and we really got shot up. The sky was almost black with bursts of flak ... Three planes were shot down which included the one directly in front of us. It went down in a ball of flames. Three chutes were sighted.

March 25: Today's mission was to Brunswick [Emden] a pretty rough target, but any oil installation is bound to be rough. Most of the Wing went after oil storage tanks, although our squadron went after the marshalling yards, and we really gave them a pasting. The squadrons that went over to Hanover must have blasted it to hell for columns of smoke were rising to 20,000 ft. Flak was very light but the 'Jets' raised cane [sic] with the formation. None of our planes were shot down but two collided in mid-air and blew up. Over Holland [the Zuider Zee] we experienced the rare and scary thrill of Red flak, but it was very light. On the whole the mission wasn't so bad. It lasted 7 hrs 30 min which is a little long. Our bomb load was 24 250 pounders.

March 30: Today's target was the submarine pens and navy yard at Wilhelmshaven. This target was first on the 'Hit' parade. Just as we were getting the feeling of a 'milk run' they threw everything they had except the kitchen sink. The flak was really intense. Our number one engine was burnt out and we received three other flak holes in the wings. The skipper brought us back safely with a lot of good flying and a little luck. This was the first time we had been hit by flak and it really had us scared.

March 31: We went to Brunswick today to smash the marshalling yards and although the flak was light it was a rough mission. Jet fighters hit the formation and knocked down one that I know of and it too blew up as it was just before 'bombs away'. Bombing was hard as we had 10/10 clouds, but one consolation it at least made the flak inaccurate. It was quite a long flight and all on oxygen which in itself tires you out. I hope we have a couple of days off now. Oh yes, our bomb load was 12 500 pounders.

Who said the war was almost over – Tell it to the Huns.

Vincent's wish was granted – his next mission was a week later, on 6 April. It had been some fortnight!

## Some Key Missions

One of the most important missions was that on the **Ploesti oil refinery**, in Wallachia, Romania. It was a key target because of the role of the refinery in supporting the German war effort; it was thought to produce up to a third of Germany's fuel. Under 'Operation Tidal Wave', five groups of B-24 Liberators were allocated the task of bombing Ploesti. Three of these groups, the 44th, 93rd and 389th, were from the 2nd Air Division stationed in Norfolk. It was too far to fly from Norfolk, and too dangerous to fly all that way across enemy territory, so the planes flew first to Libya from where the attack was made. The operation involved more than 170 B-24 Liberator bombers, which took off from temporary desert bases near Benghazi on 1 August 1943.

The lead aircraft (the B-24 *Wongo Wongo*, piloted by Lt Brian Flavelle) crashed into the sea and navigational errors meant that some aircraft took a wrong turn on approaching the target. The area was well-defended by German anti-aircraft guns, and the B-24s were without their own fighter support.

**Earl Zimmerman** (389 BG) recalled training from a base scraped out of the Libyan desert: 'We did a lot of low level flying in formation on different training flights and we wondered why low level but were never told …'

On the day, over 170 B-24s approached Ploesti, flying past Corfu, over the Pindus Mountains, Albania, and southern Yugoslavia. Carrying 500 pound bombs with 45-second delay fuses, Zimmerman's crew flew 'tail-end-Charlie', the plane at the back of the group, always the most vulnerable formation position The mission had not gone to plan. Zimmerman recalls the confusion:

As we got over Greece the five groups somehow got separated … our navigator made a wrong turn, up a range of foot hills, and by the time we had doubled back and

Ploesti, 1 August 1943.

gotten back on track we were about 45 minutes late hitting our target... We flew through fire and smoke, we were at minimum altitude, we actually had to raise up to get over some of the smoke stacks and our bombardier managed to get all of our bombs into a power house.

The attack destroyed about 40 per cent of the oil fields' capacity, but on the return flight crews came under heavy Luftwaffe fighter attack. It was the worst loss suffered by the USAAF on a single mission: over fifty aircraft were destroyed and over 500 airmen were killed or wounded, earning it the name 'Black Sunday'.

Zimmerman witnessed one of these losses:

As we came off the target there was only one other plane in front of us, it was Captain Mooney's ... He had the [landing] gear hanging and ... one engine feathered. We found out a few minutes later that Captain Mooney had been killed over the target ... Their radios had been knocked out so we had to communicate by Aldis lamp ... They asked where we were going and we told them that we would stay with them and gave them a course for Turkey.

More awards for bravery were issued for this mission than for any other mission flown by the 2nd Air Division during the Second World War. The booklet *Our Air Forces in Action* told the story of these heroes:

Aug 1 1943: Every man and every group that participated in the mission to Ploesti, Rumania, was cited for gallantry. Of all the feats of valor that day, 5 merited awarding of the nation's highest award:

Brig. Gen. (then Col.) **Leon W. Johnson** and Col. **John R. Kane** both led B-24 formations that were delivered by weather on the way to Ploesti; both arrived late and found that their objectives had already been hit by other airplanes; both were denied the element of surprise that is vital to a low-level unescorted attack.

Nazi flak was ready and Nazi fighters were in the air when Gen. Johnson and Col. Kane reached their respective targets. The refineries and tanks which they were to bomb from minimum altitude were blazing and exploding from previous attacks. Delayed action bombs, likely to explode at any moment, lay scattered through the burning rubble. Over all hung a pall of dense black smoke.

Gen. Johnson and Col. Kane attacked. Down they led their flights until flames licked at the bellies of their airplanes. Flak and fighter plane bursts whistled around them, their planes were rocked by oil exploding close below. They dropped their bombs into the inferno. Their missions were completed as planned.

Maj. **John L. Jerstad** was due for a leave after completing more than his share of missions and he was no longer connected with the group scheduled to make the attack. But he believed that his long experience would be helpful. When the crews were being picked or the Ploesti mission, he volunteered.

A burst of flak caught his plane 3 miles from the target. It began to burn immediately. Rather than jeopardize the formation he was leading by dropping out, Maj. Jerstad ignored the level landing ground below, stayed on his course. The flames in his plane spread but he managed to get his bombs away accurately. Then his plane plummeted, blazing, into the target area.

Second Lt **Lloyd H. Hughes** was in the last formation to hit the target. By the time he was ready to make his run, the Nazis had all their antiaircraft in action and the target was a seething mass of flames. Lt. Hughes came in low, dodged skilfully through barrage balloons. Then ack-ack hit his plane. Sheets of gasoline streamed from the bomb bay and left wing.

Between Lt Hughes' airplane and the target lay acres of table-top meadow. He had plenty of room and ample time to land safely. But he chose to make the bombing run.

Into the flames he piloted his Liberator, gasoline washing from its sides. When the plane came out, the left-wing was ablaze. Only then did he make an attempt to land: it was too late.

The airplane crashed and burned.

Lt. Col **Addison E. Baker's** B-24 was set afire by antiaircraft bursts 3 miles away from his objective. He could have dropped out of the formation he led and have landed in the flat country below, but he refused to place the other planes in danger by breaking formation.

With the wind-fanned planes spreading rapidly over his plane Col Baker led his flight expertly into the target. His bombs hit true. When he tried to gain sufficient altitude so that his crew could bail out, the fire ravaged plane would not respond. Skilfully, with what was left of the controls, he manoeuvred his plane out of the path of the rest of the formation.

Then the plane crashed in flames.

## 'Big Week'

By late January 1944, the combined 8th Air Force–RAF bombing offensive was in full swing. On the night of 18 January, the RAF attacked Berlin; the next day the 8th Air Force hit Frankfurt with 806 bombers escorted by 634 fighters. On 30 January, Brunswick and Hanover were attacked in strength. Between 20 and 25 February 1944, while the RAF struck German factories and defences with night assaults, the 8th Air Force delivered major blows against more than a dozen airplane factories in Germany. Simultaneously, more American planes reached up from Italy for the first time as the 15th Air Force sent bombers against Regensburg.

## D-Day

In May 1944, the 8th Air Force began a switch to tactical operations, hitting gun positions, communications targets and airfields in France and Germany helping to immobilise the German defences in preparation for the invasion of Europe. On 21 May fighters of the 8th Air Force carried out a wholesale treetop attack on

Brig.- Gen. Leon W. Johnson and Col Fred Dent holding a sash at the award of the Distinguished Unit Citation for the Ploesti mission.

Wings of friendship.

rail targets and airfields in northwestern Germany. Nearly 200 locomotives were wrecked and more than 100 enemy planes were destroyed. In June, the 8th Air Force dispatched 54,388 bombers and fighters and dropped more than 60,000 tons of bombs in strategic and tactical operations as their contribution to the invasion of Europe.

**Don Maule** (44 BG) went on his very first mission on D-Day, 6 June 1944:

We got up at 0200 and went to eat breakfast. We had fried eggs. After that we went to briefing and were told this was D-Day and we were to go to the French coast and bomb. We left at 6:30 and as we left the English coast, the water was full of boats going to France with our boys. When we got there it was cloudy so we didn't want to hit any of our own fellas. We got back at 11:45. We flew at 15,000 feet. We had twelve 500 lb bombs. No enemy fighters or flak.

On his second mission on the following day they again saw lots of boats on the Channel, and bombed a railroad center at Liscut to prevent the enemy sending troops and supplies from Paris to the coast.

The third mission, on 12 June, did not start well:

> We got up at midnight, hardly any sleep. We had hotcakes for breakfast. They were terrible as the cooks were all drunk. We went to the briefing room and everything was all mixed up as the officers had had a big dance and were all drunk. We finally found out that we were supposed to bomb a large railroad bridge in Northern France by the town Montfort. We took off at 4:30. We dropped our bombs through the clouds so we couldn't see if they hit anything. No enemy fighters or anti-aircraft fire.

General Hodges sent a message of congratulation to the men of the Second Air Division for the work they had done on D-Day. He had been told by General Doolittle that

> the ground force were most complimentary on the support they received from the Air Force and were particularly appreciative of the absence of the tragic bombing errors which it was feared might occur and which so often mar operations of this nature. The day's work reflects the greatest credit on your men. Keep it up.

Although most missions were carrying bombs, there were a few other activities that involved the men of the Second Air Division. Some planes flew **diversion flights. Delmar Johnson** described such a flight on 4 October 1944:

> We were flying a diversion over the North Sea while the B-17's were to bomb in Germany ... the object of a diversion mission is to draw some of the enemy fighter force away from the planes that are going to the target. We flew approximately northeast out of East Anglia and in due time, were to take a more easterly heading that would have us flying approximately parallel to the Frisian islands and perhaps thirty to forty miles off the German coast. We were to follow this to appoint a little

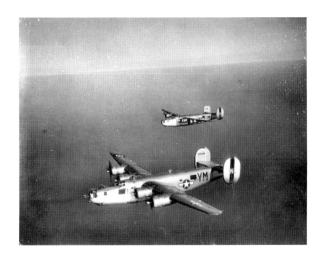

B-24 in the air.

short of Helgoland and then turn southward for a short distance in a feint toward Germany. Then when just short of the Frisians, we were to turn westward and fly again approximately parallel to the Frisians and a few miles out to sea from them, heading back toward England. Then approximately where the Holland coast turns southward we were to make another southerly feint and then return to England.

After D-Day, the bombers were sometimes used in the **support of ground troops. Ed Scamahorn**:

17 Sep: Boy oh boy something big is cooking. We were ordered out on a practice formation flight with instructions that we were to fly as low as possible and still maintain formation. We thought we did pretty good but when we landed at noon for additional briefing, Col Miller our commander said we would have to go out in the afternoon and fly lower. We did. We flew in formation at nearly deck level. We pulled up for trees, fences, church steeples etc. We tipped over sailboats and scared hundreds of otherwise happy English who were out enjoying the sunshine. Most of them wave when they see us coming then duck when they realize how low we really are. It was hard on livestock as they were badly frightened by our sudden appearance and many of them ran crazily into fences and buildings.

18 Sep: Well, today it happened. We delivered the goods to paratroopers and glider borne troops that had just landed in Holland. We dropped bundles by parachute and free fall from 350 to 500 ft altitude. We flew into the drop area at the lowest possible altitude to prevent the Jerries using the deadly 888s to any extent. We had to pull up to make the drop and then immediately drop back down to deck level to come out. Our plane was hit by machine gun fire from the ground troops and we were in pretty bad shape for awhile. The slugs took out the entire hydraulic system and nearly severed the rudder and elevator cables. What a war, the Dutch waving to us on one side and the Germans shooting at us from the other and we can't hit back (orders) for fear of shooting the Dutch.

Other missions were by **Carpetbaggers**: Specialised crews that began flying at low level, dropping propaganda leaflets, espionage agents and supplies for resistance groups, and retrieved airmen interned in Sweden. The ball turret on their B24s was replaced with a ring known as a 'Joe-hole' for dispensing the leaflets – and the agents! They flew from bases all over Britain, including Watton and Metfield. Over 4,000 passengers were brought back to the UK from Sweden between April 1944 and June 1945, including American airmen, Norwegians escaping to carry on the struggle against the Nazis, and people of at least six other nationalities.

## Completing the Missions

The men were committed to flying a set number of missions, twenty-five at first, rising by stages to thirty-five.

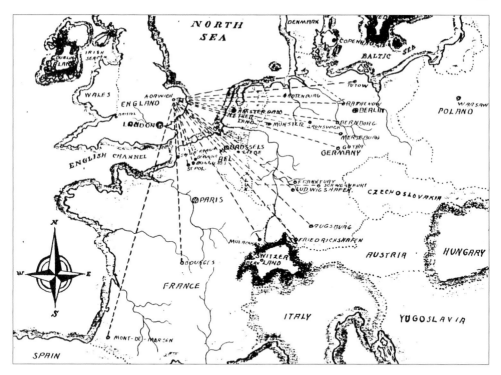

Map showing typical missions undertaken by a crew (Ray Waters)

Naturally, people looked forward to completing their 'tour'.
**Robert Boyle:**

13 Aug '44: Tonight I feel as though the weight of the world has been lifted from my shoulders. I finally am able to say 'Stop worrying – I'm done'. I finished up my 32nd mission which constitutes a combat tour. It's really a great feeling to know I won't be giving those guys a chance to shoot at me anymore. We are all very thankful to have finished up with no one on the crew hurt.

27 Aug '44: I am being assigned to HQ's Sqdn, and accordingly I had to move from the 847th Sqdn area to the quarters where all the 'paddlefeet', or ground officers, live. I am now a paddlefoot too ... It is much nicer than before. We lived in a Nissen hut (you've probably seen pictures of them). Now I live in an old mansion, and was very fortunate in getting a room rather than a dormitory ... I am assigned to the Group Training Office, as an instructor-pilot. That in itself doesn't require much effort, as we rarely have much in the way of practice flights requiring instructors. Therefore, each of us assume other duties also. I am the Synthetic Trainer officer, which means I keep all our trainers operating, and see that the instructors are kept up upon the latest information. It's rather interesting, and yet doesn't take up too much effort either.

**Curtis Anderson:**

> 4 Nov '44. I'm just living for the end of the mission. More talk about us having to do 35, hope it's just a rumour.
>
> 27 Dec '44: today is my red letter day in the E. T. O., my last one. Target Nuenkirchen, marshalling yards. Just two bursts of flak I could hear, plenty we could see, but that was enough to hear. I was really sweating the landing. Three passes at the field before we landed #35. Next day: a night of rest and I feel like a million. Did a little detail this afternoon, wired Mose the good news. Bill and the boys finished today, they had a party and I went over for a while. A drunk outfit!

Just two days later Anderson was told he had been selected to go to Hethel and fly relay and weather ships. He was unimpressed: 'what a place, a mess if I have ever seen one. Barracks crowded and stuff all over the place. I feel like a rookie with all my stuff and no place to put it.'

## Fighters

The bombers were supported by fighters. During the Second World War, the 65th Fighter Wing's main role was to escort bombers attacking industrial targets, weapons

Alden E. Smith, fighter pilot, in his aircraft.

sites and transport networks in Europe. They also strafed [flew low and used their machine guns], attacking enemy airfields and other targets. A typical fighter group had three fighter squadrons of about thirty aircraft. The 65th Fighter Wing mostly flew P-51 'Mustangs' or P-47 'Thunderbolts'. They were very different machines to the bombers, with just one person on board and a speed of between 430 and 440 mph. The P-47 had a range of 790 miles, the P-51 a range of 950 miles, so that they could not accompany the bombers all the way on a long raid; beyond a certain distance the bombers were on their own. As of October 1944, there were six fighter bases assigned to the 2nd Air Division: Saffron Walden, Debden, Boxted, Steeple Morden, Bottisham (or Little Walden) and Wattisham.

The most successful fighter group was 56 FG. They arrived at Horsham in April 1943 and were based at Halesworth (Holton) airfield from July 1943 to April 1944, when they moved to Boxted, near Sudbury. The group used Thunderbolts and became known as 'Zemke's Wolfpack' after their commander, Col Hubert Zemke. They were the top scoring fighter group in the 8th Air Force, with over 650 air-to-air victories. A total of forty-nine men in the group earned the title 'Ace'.

**'Andy' Anderson** (458 BG):

Fighters knocked down 3 of our bombers so fast we didn't know what hit us, we were lucky! A B-24 spinning down is not a pleasant sight. One blew up, 1 chute about 15 from the other two, maybe more, I hope so. 4 '51s' drove one 190 into the ground, those fighter pilots are a blood-thirsty lot. And am I glad to see them around, they truly are our 'Little Friends'

**James Chew** (56 FG):

Our fighter planes were the Republic P-47s. They were named Thunderbolts. There were a total of eight 50-caliber machine guns on each airplane – four in each wing. These planes were high altitude Fighters, and were designed to cover our Bombers over Enemy Territory during Bombing Missions. They had a four-bladed propeller, powered by an 18-cylinder Pratt & Whitney engine. They were veritable flying destroyers, and could also be used for Bombing Missions of their own, and so were designed to carry a 500-pound bomb under each wing, plus extra fuel tanks that could be jettisoned during flight.

## Rodney Ives and Douglas Pleasant

Memoirs are by definition written by survivors, but letters written in England by some men who were later to be killed in action provide a poignant memento of sacrifices made in wartime. In November 1943, **Rodney Ives** (453 BG) wrote home to his mother: 'I wanted to get word to you so there would be nothing to worry about. I haven't the exact things I want to get you & Dad for Christmas so they'll probably be late.'

He wrote home in January 1944:

Please send 50 dollars. Am having a wonderful time, only young once. Seriously though, I've been studying the English customs a little too freely and I'll be a little short this month. With this $50 though I think I can stay ahead of the game because after I start operations I probably won't have so much time to complete my survey of English reactions to Yanks.

I've been having a swell time in the E.T.O. and the English treat you swell except for prices. There are two prices – English and Yank. We haven't been assigned to our permanent outfit as yet but we should be shortly and I am really anxious to get going. I've met another of my classmates who is an instructor here and he's finished his missions. We had a swell time talking over the old days at Hondo and I found that most of my class are either a prisoner of war or lost. The ones that are left are all captains. Do you remember Ken Dougherty who called me up from Portland when I was home after I graduated. He's a prisoner of war in Germany.

I've seen quite a bit of England so far but I haven't hit any big towns like London as yet. I'm not supposed to voice any position about the English people but the countryside is a lot like the New England States and in most towns the population is very crowded – with many tenement sections. All of the richer people live in large country homes. There doesn't seem to be much of a middle class here – either rich or poor. There are plenty of pubs (bars) and I'm getting so I like their warm beer – no hard liquor. There are no nite clubs except in London which has become Americanized – at least that's what I've been told.

Our quarters are Nissen huts at this station but they're pretty comfortable in spite of their looks. The food is excellent and we have plenty of laughs with Captain York around. I guess I've never told you about him. He was with us at Tonopah and Mountain Home and he brought an instructor crew over with us. He used to be a college football player – a great big lunk – but pretty intelligent. He's a typical college Joe and he can really keep you laughing.

Well there isn't much more of importance right now Mom but I found out for sure that I'll be able to write to you about the missions so you'll be able to sweat them out with me when I start operations. I guess you get kind of lonesome but keep your chin up and I'll be home one of these days – maybe sooner than you think.

P.S. About the money be sure and take it out of my account – I don't know the procedure for sending it but use the same as you did with Dave's.

Other letters followed, describing his experiences:

We are flying deputy lead on every mission these days. This means that we might take over at any time if the leader is shot down or has a mechanical failure. We have to do this for quite a few missions before we start leading ourselves but it is good practice.

It was a target in Germany again and it was our toughest mission to date. In the first place we had to get up where the temperature was 40 degrees below and then we got hit over the target. We ended up with 25 holes in our ship and two men slightly injured … Everyone took it damn good today and I think everyone was scared – I know I was – but I kept working and now after a hot shower and a drink it's a long way off.'

Rodney Ives never made it home and was never to receive a reply to his last letter to his mother, postmarked 26 November 1944. On that day he was a senior navigator in Captain Ray Conard's crew, which set off on a mission to bomb a railway viaduct outside Bielefeld. The plane crashed at Kenninghall just a few miles from their airbase. Conard was posthumously awarded the Distinguished Service Cross for crashing the aircraft so as to avoid striking nearby houses.

**Douglas Pleasant** (492 BG) also wrote letters home to his mother:

> May 8 1944. The bag that was shipped across for me got here at last but some so-and-so removed a quart of bonded whiskey, all the candy and all but one package of gum. Good thing I have a few packs of gum here now as it keeps your ears cleared when descending from altitude and keeps or helps keep your nerves settled.
> May 19 1944: So far I haven't been out of camp though we can now get passes. Will tell you all I find out about England when I do, I hear the beer is vile and their stronger drink worse; ice cream and cold drinks nonexistent.
> May 28 1944: Went to town a few nights ago. Can't name the town but it's about three miles and I had to walk both ways. Had two glasses of ale – the English equivalent of beer – but couldn't get a thing to eat. Got a snack in the mess hall and saw part of the movie *The Fleet's In* – the projector broke down.
> June 4 1944: The most popular English beverage – to wit, mild and bitter (an ale) has many uses. One of these is as a paint thinner (joke).

Waiting for the return.

June 29 1944: You may wonder as to why you have not heard from me lately. The censors, I understand, are holding up all mail from over here until things on the Continent are firmly established. This letter should not be delayed very much, I hope. Am well, get better food now, but am not getting too much sleep. We now get steaks, pork chops, fresh eggs and the like two, three and sometimes four times a week. Had pork chops tonight....[On same letter] July 3 1944: Was slightly interrupted in the writing of this letter due to unforeseen circumstances. Everything is now normal. I had a two day pass come up suddenly and had to dash to make my connection to a town. Had a swell time seeing the sights and talking to the natives. Sure hungry when I got back. These English people seem to think we can live indefinitely on tarts, tea and cheese sandwiches. Steak for supper tonight and I have my plate out for seconds before I get to the mess hall... Even on pass your money is little good here. Spent less than three pounds ($12) in the two days. Now have 43 pounds and some change, but am keeping it here as we will finish our tour of duty in two or three months, I think, and may get a chance to tour England and pick up a few knickknacks.

Pleasant's last known letter was written the following day, 4 July, to friends at the *St Louis Globe-Democrat* newspaper, where he had worked before enlisting. He was reported missing in action on 7 July 1944 when the bomber in which was flying was attacked by enemy fighters near Bernburg. In 1947, 7 July 1944 was confirmed as the date of his death.

# Chapter Four

# Killed or Missing

The casualty rate among these young airmen was very high. At one stage, one man in three was becoming a casualty before the completion of their missions. The loss of comrades inevitably had a sobering effect upon the survivors.

**Calvin H. Hanlyn** (446 BG):

The war has finally hit home to me and hard. The barracks is quiet tonight, quiet because eight men didn't come back today. The raid was Osnabruck and they met plenty of opposition. It happened so fast, it's hard for me to realize that three crews are gone. In the corner is Jake's [Sydney C. Jacobson] bunk, blankets, mess gear, flying equipment, everything just as he left it this morning. Jake was one of the best pilots I've ever flown with and his navigator was my best friend. Next to mine is Jack's bunk [Otis K. Cranford]. That's the way it was with us. We liked each other's company and went everywhere together, like Abbott and Costello … Never a thought of not coming back, it was understood that together we would tear LA apart after our tour was completed. I tell you, it doesn't pay to make a friendship like ours.

**Eddie Albers** (492 BG):

There are only four of us left out of twelve who bunked in this hut. Many more of the huts are completely empty tonight. Words alone can't express how it feels to know they won't come back. The hut seems so empty and quiet tonight … Soon the boys' things will be picked up and turned into supply and all personal things sent home. I can realise how all the relatives are going to feel to hear the sad news.

Inevitably not everyone behaved with that much dignity. **Willard Bristling** (492 BG) remembered 'the predatory attitudes of remaining crews who came in when a crew was shot down and stole the dead's remaining property'.

There were many places where a plane and its crew might come down, and this would make all the difference to the fate of those who survived the crash: in England, into the sea, in a friendly country, in a neutral country or in occupied territory. Each had its own problems.

# Crash Landings in England

**Calvin Hanlyn:**

It began like all the rest as Jack and I slopped through the ever present mud on our way to breakfast. It was just another cold, miserable dawn, and as usual we were very frank in expressing our opinion of dear old England. As we fly at every opportunity, there was nothing unusual about the training flight scheduled for 11:00. It was to be a high altitude mission with the temperature around −35 degrees Centigrade. Cold as hell!

However, the landing was dramatic:

I am on the flight deck looking out of the window when he [the pilot] begins the approach and it looks as though we are coming in too high. A glance at the air speed meter shows us making 140 mph (miles per hour) which is too hot for this particular ship. As we flash over the fence, which marks the southern end of the runway, we are still indicating 125 mph and I can't see how in the hell he expects to set her down on the first third. Now we are at the half way mark and our wheels still haven't touched the runway. By now I'm bitching because we will have to go around and make another approach, this will take at least five minutes and I'm really hungry. I'm expecting to hear the roar of engines any second now as the pilot opens the throttle and all that. But nothing happens. I jump up and look forward just as he is about to set us down with only 100 yards of strip left. With a warning yelp, I dive for my crash position, just as we hit the runway. Trying frantically to check our wild plunge, the pilot locks the brakes, this was like trying to stop a Kodiak bear with a pea shooter. So at a cool 90 miles an hour we take off on a cross-country that I'm not likely to forget. When everything but the putt-putt had either been torn off by trees and grazing cows or smashed beyond recognition, we came to a smashing stop. I tore open the hatch, nearly broke both legs in plunging 13 feet to the dear old earth, and took off like a P51. I mean I got out of that smoking wreck in a hell of a hurry.

Extract from the mission diary of **Fred Bechetti** (445 BG):

July 31 (Monday): Up at 02:30 and takeoff at 09:00 for a target at Ludwigshaven, Germany. While in the assembly over Tibenham, at 16,000 feet, our No. 4 prop ran away. We feathered it and announced that we were aborting the mission. We were carrying armed fragmentation bombs, so we had to fly out over the Channel to a precise latitude/longitude to drop the bombs. I gave a heading and we proceeded to the drop point, losing altitude at the rate of 300 ft per minute. We turned for Tibenham after dropping the bombs, losing altitude rapidly. Threw out everything heavy – flak suits, ammo and even the generator. About a 500 ft ceiling under us, so that we could not see the ground. When we felt we were over land, according to our navigation, we voted to bail out. We were at only 1500 ft over England! I went back to the rear hatch to supervise the bailing out. McGovern went out first (He fractured his tibia on landing). Sherrick was second (He landed OK). Sladovnik was third (He broke his left leg). Smith next (He sprained his right ankle landing in a WAAF field, where the women took care of him splendidly). Goldstein was next (He landed OK). McHenry next (He sprained his right angle). I went out last, while Bolton and Palmer, with a lightened ship, were able to land at Tibenham. I landed in a victory garden of a house in the suburbs of Norwich next to the home of Mr Morris, at 185, Newmarket Road. Mr Morris treated me like a king, giving me a scotch and soda; although the British Bobbies who came cycling up later were a little suspicious of me, especially with an Italian name. The American MPs [Military Policemen] came to take me back in a jeep. The Lord was really with us this time!

## Ed Scamahorn:

We had to leave the formation as we were having considerable difficulty and couldn't keep up with the others. When we got to home field we found that we could not get the landing gear down and had no brakes or flaps. We were also afraid that the rudder and elevator controls might go out at any time as there were only a few strands holding the cables together. Home field sent us away as they didn't want any wreckage blocking the runway so that other planes could not land. We then went to Woodbridge, a special field designed for the landing of damaged aircraft. The runway is about 2 miles long and several hundred feet wide. Capt Bridges had about the same trouble as we did and had landed his plane just before our arrival. He and his crew managed to get out safely but his plane was burning in the center of the runway and we were told to circle the field and wait for clearance. After about one hour we received clearance to land and it was a good thing as we were running very low on gasoline. Sgt Armstrong, our engineer, had been working on the landing gear manually. He had managed to get the nose wheel and the right main down but couldn't do anything with the left main gear. We had to land as the fuel tanks were showing empty. The left main gear was hanging down limply, not in place or locked. As we touched down, I applied a little more power to no 1 engine in hopes that would help hold the left wing up as we lost speed, that didn't do much good. The left gear folded almost immediately and allowed the no 1 prop to hit the runway turning at a high rate of speed. As soon as the prop hit the asphalt, it snapped the crankshaft and bounced about 20 ft in the air spinning rapidly and flying forward parallel to our aircraft. The drag of the left wing on the pavement caused our plane to veer sharply to the left and this tuned us into the path of the rapidly spinning prop which was moving at our same rate of speed. I could see the spinning prop out of the corner of my eye and much more clearly as it sliced through the nose section like a buzz saw just inches in front of my feet.

As the plane skidded along on its belly, the hydraulic and probably some gasoline from broken lines caught fire. Sgt Dzik, one of the waist gunners, saw the flames and jumped out of the rear escape hatch. We must have been going close to fifty miles an hour at the time he jumped. He had rolled end over end for quite a way and he looked like a native American had practised scalping on his head. He was cut up and badly bruised when the ambulance delivered him to the rest of us. He had disobeyed instructions so he didn't get much sympathy from me. He could have easily been killed. All of the other crewmen had escaped any injury. I had given orders that no one was to leave from their braced positions until the plane had come to a complete stop. The plane was totally destroyed. We were shortly picked up in an army 2½ ton truck and on our way back to North Pickenham. The ride was very cold so we popped open some parachutes that we had salvaged and wrapped up in the nylon.

Some planes came down in built-up areas, which could cause loss of life on the ground. At least one crew sacrificed their lives to avoid killing civilians. Several poignant letters were sent to **Jordan Uttal**, stationed at the 2nd Air Division's Headquarters, Ketteringham Hall, expressing sympathy when the B-24 *Lady Jane* struck the tower of St Philip's church, Heigham, and crashed in the Corporation Yard, off Barker Street, two miles from the 458th Bomb Group's runway at Horsham St Faith. All nine crew members on board were killed in the crash: Ralph Dooley (pilot), Arthur Akin (stand-in co-pilot), Paul Gorman (navigator), John Jones (engineer and top-turret operator), Paul Wadsworth (radio operator), Oscar Nelson and Don Quirk (waist-gunners), John Philips (nose-gunner) and Ralph Von Bergen (tail-gunner).

Mrs Bates of Heigham Street, Norwich: 'I am writing on behalf of the Residents of Heigham in which your gallant men lost their lives in saving us through their plane crashing. We have gathered round for them as a token of respect.'

Mrs Paynter of Heigham Street: 'I feel that I must just put on record our very grateful thanks for the big sacrifice made by the noble crew of the airplane that crashed so near here on Friday last. We all feel that in the way they manoeuvred the machine they gave their lives for ours.'

Mrs Brett of Wroxham Road:

I have hesitated to intrude earlier to pay a personal tribute to the brave lads who gave up their lives so nobly to save their friends and allies recently. I had just left the Lazar House on Sprowston Rd & noticed the bomber flying very low. At first I did not realise any danger, so fascinated was I in watching the skill of the pilot & his efforts to gain height. A girl just passing me with a pram screamed, 'it's coming down, run'. Snatching her baby out of the pram, she ran up an opening, the pram meanwhile trickling into the gutter (which I hope she retrieved). Watching it out of sight I breathed a silent prayer for its safe landing & a 'thank you' to the crew. Later, calling on a dear friend, an invalid of years, I found her very distressed, saying she had been so frightened she had forgotten to pray. Lying in bed near her open window she felt sure it must have come into the room. Otherwise, she always breathed a prayer when hearing them go over, as we all do … and also to send up a prayer for their safe return, whether our own boys, USA or any other ally.

Despite such heroism on the part of the American airmen, it was inevitable that there would be the occasional fatal incident. On 14 January 1945 a B-24 touched the gable end of a house in Spinke Road, Norwich, and came down, killing two children who were among a group playing in the garden. One of the first people on the scene was Earl Zimmerman, actually in the next house where he had been having tea with the family of his English fiancée. He helped pull two boys out of the wreckage, but one of them, eleven-year-old Bryan Jones, died. The other fatality was Mary Kemp, aged five.

## Into the North Sea

One important job of the fighters was to rescue men who had come down in the North Sea. Brigadier General Jesse Auton wrote:

> The 65th Fighter Wing has had a vital part in the control of every 8th Air Force mission since the Fourth of July 1943. A constant phase of this control has been for Air/Sea Rescue. The many loyal men who have labored unceasingly to make rescue more swift and sure deserve great credit for making what is certain to be a lasting contribution to the safety of air operations, civil as well as military. They have saved a great number of lives, shepherding hundreds of hurt aircraft safely home to England and bringing back nearly a thousand men lost at sea.

This is a typical rescue report:

> 20 July 1944, Bomber N for Nan called at 1414 hours, when in the vicinity of Knocke at 6700 feet with two engines out and a third giving trouble. He was given a vector of 280 degrees to Manston but apparently did not have sufficient control to fly the vector exactly. The bomber crossed out the enemy coast shortly after the first fix and lost altitude so rapidly it was impossible to fix it again (because of the 'line-of-sight') other than a one-string bearing of 097 degrees. N ditched at 1428 hours.
> Teamwork aircraft were in the general area at the time, but could not locate the bomber before it hit the water. The area was searched thoroughly by three Hudsons and four Teamwork spotters for three hours without success. Another group of five Warwicks searched to the north, and six more P-47's covered to the south, in addition to two HSL's patrolling the area.
> The search continued at 0530 hours, 21 July, and a Warwick found two dinghies with nine men, 20 miles due north of Dunkirk. An airborne lifeboat was dropped, and all nine men transferred to it from the dinghies. Two HSL's from Dover picked them up 17 miles north of Dunkirk, and all were in good shape. Teamwork aircraft provided cover. Weather conditions were very bad and everyone concerned did an excellent piece of work.

**Charles Trout** (492 BG) was one who bailed out into the North Sea, from a stricken plane:

> I dived from the plane as though I was diving into water. When the slipstream hit me it took my breath and threw me around pretty rough. When I was low enough for

Demonstrating a liferaft.

clearance and everything got so quiet, I pulled the ripcord but nothing happened. The chute didn't open! I reached in and pulled the pilot chute out. Everything came out of the pack and I stopped with a sudden jerk, looked up and was very pleased to see that nice white parachute above me… I looked down and seemed to be about 100 feet above the sea but hit very quickly, a second or two later. Don't know how far I went under but came up immediately. When the cold water got through my clothes it took my breath. I struggled for about ten minutes before I finally got my breath back as the waves were breaking right over the top of me. I unbuckled my chute harness and thought I was rid of it.

**Bill Long** (392 BG) was another whose plane ditched into the North Sea. He recalled that the seven crew members at the rear of the plane 'just fell into the water', but the three in the pilot's compartment had to smash their way out. He commented that the water was so cold – even in September – that the men would only have lasted twenty minutes or so. Fortunately, the British Air Sea Rescue soon picked up their radio signal. They dropped a small launch, which none of the men could reach, and then a life raft. Three of the men managed to get onto the raft, and hauled in all the other men in the water around them. Two were already missing. A British Air Sea

Rescue launch soon arrived and picked them up. They circled the area but could not find the other two men. Eventually they had to give them up as lost and head back to Yarmouth.

Airmen who ditched into the sea and had to swim until they were rescued were entitled to membership of what was known as the 'Goldfish Club'!

## Friendly Countries

Before D-Day, the whole of Western Europe was controlled by the Nazis and the only escape for a stricken plane was to a neutral country on the fringe of that evil empire. After D-Day, as the Allies advanced across France and eventually into Luxembourg, Belgium and Holland, there was always the possibility of an emergency landing at a friendly airport for refuelling and patching up ready for the journey back to England, or of parachuting from a stricken plane into the hands of friends.

**Lyndon Crane Allen** (44 BG):

Our 21st and 22nd missions were especially interesting. Both were flown on the two days before Christmas 1944 in support of the ground troops during the Battle of the Bulge. On our 21st we had 25 minutes of continuous flak which was quite intense and accurate, but I do remember how beautiful the landscape was completely covered with snow ... Then on our 22nd mission, the day before Christmas, it was an all out effort of the 8th Air Force, again in support of the ground troops. Our plane had been test flown after repairs the day before and the fuel had not been topped off after the test flight; our engineer found out that we were almost out of fuel right after we turned from the target. So our pilot had to hurriedly find a field for us to make an emergency landing. In making the approach to the fighter strip that he located I thought we were about to spin in and crash so I started to bail out at around 700 feet. Fortunately one of the waist gunners grabbed my parachute harness and held me back. We were so low on gas that Struthers had only one engine left with which to taxi after landing. Struthers was told that the German tanks were only 5 miles east of the field, but the field was being evacuated and we had to get out as fast as possible. That we did just as soon as we refuelled. It was the most unusual Christmas Eve that I have ever spent.

## Neutral Countries – Internment

During the Second World War, 167 American bomber crews landed in Switzerland, Sweden or Turkey. The men were interned, which normally meant staying in that country for the duration of the war – although several did manage to escape in time to return to duty.

After the Ploesti mission, seventy-eight crewmen were interned in Turkey, including **Earl Zimmerman**, radio operator on Lt James' crew, which was forced by Turkish fighters to land in a cornfield near Ismir. In his memoirs, Zimmerman describes life as an internee, including playing chess with Russian and German deserters. Under laws of international warfare, internees caught attempting to escape could be treated severely. 'About ten or fifteen of us started the fight in the hallway and when the guards came to see what was happening everyone took off for the hills. I understand that two or three were caught down by the Syrian border and returned.'

Eventually, Zimmerman escaped to England via Syria, Cairo, where he toured the pyramids and sphinx, and Marrakech, where he met General Montgomery. He remembered:

> I escaped with a bunch of the boys and we went to the railroad station ... We had been given money and phoney passports ... I noticed as we pulled out the Turkish major was standing on the platform saluting. I think someone was paid off somewhere along the line.

After his escape, Zimmerman was transferred to RAF Leuchars, Scotland, for Operation Ball (night flying black Liberators over Norway to supply the underground) before returning to his airbase at Hethel, Norfolk.

Most American airmen were interned in Switzerland. Following a mission targeting a fighter plant at Lechfeld, Germany, on 13 April 1944, **Forrest Clark**, radio operator on Rockford C. Griffith's crew, was interned at Adleboden. In December 1944, after eight months internment, Clark escaped across the French border during the Battle of the Bulge:

> We edged closer and closer to the barbed wire. Each lay on the cold icy ground, full out, squirming forward with our legs on the ice-encrusted snow ... I ran until I gained the front door of the farmhouse. Someone knocked softly. An upper window flew open and a head appeared ... It was the most welcome light we had seen for four days and nights during our long cold walk over the mountains.

Having travelled through a sniper holdout pocket and area of land mines, Clark met a United States Seventh Army patrol, returning to his base at Shipdham, Norfolk, just after Christmas, 1944.

On 20 June 1944, the 8th Air Force undertook a mission to Politz, an oil refinery near Stettin in Poland, close to the Baltic coast. Thirteen planes of 492 BG were lost under heavy flak and enemy fighter attack. Several planes exploded in mid-air killing all the crew instantaneously. Several badly damaged planes made it across the Baltic to Malmo, including the commanding officer, **John Lossee:**

> We arrived over Malmo airport, a grass field fighter base, boasting of an 18 inch hay crop. We cranked the gear down and 20 degrees of flak. We landed without hydraulics, no brakes. We were on a collision course with another parked aircraft and a hangar. At what seemed to be the last moment before crashing, the aircraft turned 90 degrees left and skidded to an abrupt stop on still dewy grass, thanks to a shot out left tyre. There were some dozen aircraft that made it into Sweden

that day. We were all marched to the local bastille that evening and formally interned.

The plane piloted by **Elvern Seltzinger** also made it to Sweden: 'We crossed the Swedish coast near Ystano at about 15,000 feet … About that time three Swedish fighters came up and escorted us to the field.'

They landed with great difficulty due to damage to the plane's landing gear, and were promptly arrested. Seltzinger recalled:

> Later in the day we were marched to the local jail where we spent one night and next day we were moved by train to Falun. We spent two or three nights in this barbed wire stockade and were interviewed by members of the American Embassy. We were moved by bus to Ratvik, where I was to spend the next four months at Pensionnat Ledalshoiden. During the night of 7 November 1944 I was flown from Stockholm to Scotland, then down to England and then onto New York City on 3 December 1944. Some of the crew came back with me and some who were working in the Embassy or reprocessing airplanes remained there until the following year.

## Capture

Regulations were issued as to what to do if captured by the enemy:

> **When You Are Overseas**
> **Capture:**
>
> Most enemy intelligence comes from prisoners. If captured, you are required to give only three facts: *Your Name, Your Grade, Your Army Serial Number*. Don't talk, don't try to fake stories, and use every effort to destroy all papers. When you are going into an area where capture is possible carry only essential papers and plan to destroy them prior to capture if possible. Do not carry personal letters about your person; they tell much about you, and the envelope has on it your unit and organization.
>
> *Be Sensible; Use Your Head*

Some crew members came down with their planes; others escaped a doomed plane by parachute.

**Milton Goodridge** (492 BG) went down over the Baltic:

> I went back to try to get the plane level but no such luck. The next thing I knew I wasn't in the plane anymore and pulled the ripcord on the chute and it opened. The plane had evidently blown up and blew me out of it. When the chute opened debris from the plane fell by me, but fortunately none hit me or the chute. On the way down I saw two or three other chutes below me, one of which burst into flames as I watched

Ben Madamba       Miller       Jack feingold

Whitfield Brooke       George Harlow

Pictures to be used in case of capture.

it ... I hit the water and got out of my chute, inflated the Mae West. I could see land and started to swim for it, but it seemed like I was making very little progress. I passed out and when I came to I was on the deck of a German boat.

**Merrill Olson** (389 BG):

A parachute jump is not a fearful thing as most people would believe. The first sensation is a terrific rush of air and speed. When that is gone there descends upon you a sudden and awe-inspiring silence and a calm peaceful sense of floating through space ... I could hear the gulls screaming as they flew by me and could hear the quaint Dutch windmills squeak as their blades turned in the autumn breeze.

He was found by Dutch civilians, who tried to help him evade capture, but was captured when he tried to break through German lines in company with the Dutchmen and a Canadian sergeant. Because he was wearing civilian clothes he was interrogated and told he could be shot as a spy, and suffered several days solitary confinement in Rotterdam, writing later:

Have you ever been alone? You will say yes, no doubt, but stop for a moment and consider the full significance of the word 'alone'. Alone in a strange land, thousands of miles away from home and friends; in the hands of a ruthless gang of criminals, the full story of their abominable deeds just now coming to light. Alone in a cell, four by eight, never speaking to a living soul, or hearing or seeing a civilised person ... Ten days I spent in that hole.

For these men, getting one's surrender was not always easy. Local civilians or SS officers, stirred up by propaganda about American 'terror flyers', might beat or even kill their prisoners. **Ken Dougherty** (389 BG) saw four American airmen hanging from a tree: they had been lynched. As a prisoner he was subjected to a terrifying ordeal, being paraded in public:

As soon as we got to the crowded part of the walk they forced me into the gutter and put one guard in front of me and another behind me with the third one on the side walk. They then started saying, all three of them and pointing at me, '*Americanishe Officer Flieger Kaput*' [sic]. They kept this up for about 6 or 8 blocks until we came to a large cul-de-sac paved with cobblestones in front of the RR station. By then they had created quite a stir and there was a 'mob' forming. There were a great many people and they were getting really wrought up and started to go for me.

The Germans cocked their guns and ordered the crowd to halt, taking Dougherty back to prison: 'the cell needless to say looked and felt good.'

For these men, the war was indeed over. The rest of it would have to be spent in a prisoner of war camp. With German citizens on an almost starvation diet, it was inevitable that prisoners would be very poorly fed. Dougherty remembered how welcome Red Cross parcels were:

Each parcel contained eleven pounds of food and the Germans supplemented it with a loaf of 'heavy' bread. The black stuff and the supplies were such that we were allowed a full or ½ package so there were about 12 to 16 men in a room in a barracks type building and all the Airmen who didn't know how to cook. The Germans also gave us some potatoes and some barley flour so naturally the main topic was food. For a few days it was unorganized and we were not getting the best out of it so each fellow had to take his turn as 'chef' and we cooked on a communal wood stove. The barracks had about 10 rooms occupied by 150 to 175 people so each room was allowed to use the stove or share it. On my turn to cook I remembered the scalloped potatoes routine I watched my mother perform so with the powdered milk, cheese, spam and whatever else I could get out of the Red Cross parcel I made a '*Kriege* stew' and it really put the stretch on the food supply and instead of lying awake hungry that night everyone felt good. Well fed for the first time. Needless to say, the idea of '*Kriege* stew' spread so then we started making all sorts of pans and cooking utensils out of the tin cans and the eating situation was turned around. There was a central kitchen and other packages and supplies would come into the camp so that in the central kitchen cake mixes would be baked, etc.

Some of the rations provided, as a matter of fact almost all the provisions brought to us by the Germans, except our Red Cross parcels, was bad food. It is surprising how rugged a human stomach or digestive system is. I remembered the pea soup we had so often. All the peas had weevils in them and they floated to the top of the cooking vat and they would skim a lot of them off ... Then there was the '*Blutworst*' and if you weren't hungry the sight of it, lone, would make you want to vomit. I really think that was the hardest meal I ever ate. You just can't believe ... The Red Cross parcels were not delivered many times and regular eating habits simply disappeared. At best we got 1 meal per day.

As the liberating armies advanced upon Germany from west and east, the Germans retreated into their heartland. They often took their prisoners with them, forcing them to make the series of enforced movements known as 'The Long March'. **Merrill Olson** was at a camp near Nurnberg and was among 10,000 prisoners force-marched to Moosburg, a distance of ninety miles:

We had all made some sort of make-shift pack to carry what food we had and our blankets and personal belongings. Some had manufactured two-wheeled and four-wheeled carts and we must have been quite a humorous sight as we marched out the gate. The march turned out to be a farce. After the first day, the guards lost all control or discipline over us. We didn't keep in column and most of us wandered the roads on our own and took our own good time about it. There were little or no German rations handed out on the march. We did get Red Cross parcels every third day. We saved the cigarettes and soap from these and traded with German civilians along the way for bread, potatoes, eggs, onions and all sorts of foodstuffs ... At night the Germans would stop us in some small town and we would sleep in the barns ... There were Americans strung out for twenty or thirty miles along the road. The guards had given up trying to keep us in order. Every few miles they would have a round-up and put us in a group of one hundred or so and started marching us on. The first woods we came to we ducked in and waited until the column was past and then started out alone again. After ten days and nights of this we arrived at the new camp in Moosburg, in much better physical and mental shape than we were on leaving Nurnberg.

# Chapter Five

# Daily Life on the Bases

## The Huts

**Ken Jones:**

Arriving at the railroad station at Diss from the replacement depot we were loaded on 6×6 trucks and were driven to Hethel airbase near Norwich England. Our footlockers would not follow us for two more weeks. Upon arrival at the 389th Bomb Group [base], the enlisted men were taken to their squadron area and the commissioned officers to quarters in a Nissen hut. We settled in and were introduced to flyers sharing these quarters. The routine was explained; location of the mess hall, one scuttle of coal a day for an extremely small stove (which doesn't burn all night), no hot water for shaving (heat water on the stove). Each hut was issued a machete to chop up cardboard bomb rings for extra fuel. Exposed to the outside weather elements and partially enclosed were shower stalls with no hot water. Dry cleaned clothing came back smelling like 100 octane gas. Laundry service wasn't bad. Issued PX cards [Post Exchange, the base 'shop'] for rationed toiletry and other sundries. GI bunk beds. We were cautioned to shave before every mission or the face would be rubbed raw by the oxygen mask.

**Lyndon Allen:**

Now about my life in England. The enlisted men in our crew stayed in two different Quonset huts: McDonald, Jacobs and Carpenter were in one, Grif and I in another. Naturally the officers were in their own hut. I don't remember just how many men were in our hut, I think between 16 and 20, half of them along each side of the hut. There were never the enlisted men of one complete crew in our hut. We had a typical pot-bellied coal stove in the centre of our hut and were issued a certain amount of coal each week. However the coal pile was not far away from our hut behind a fence that didn't stop us adding to our weekly ration, periodically. The floor was concrete, a crumbling type that could never be kept clean. We had English type mattresses on our cot, three biscuits that were the hardest and lumpiest thing that I ever slept on – our conclusion was that they were filled with rubble from the bombings in London! As typical GIs we griped about a number of things but were really very happy to have the

Hut exterior (Ray Waters).

things as they were. We knew that our beds would be dry every night, something that the infantry knew nothing about.

**Willis Marshall:**

When we arrived at Hethel, home of the 389th, we were assigned to a barracks. We found this to be a pretty much pristine living condition but a castle compared to the GIs on the ground in Europe. We found we had to sleep on cots with three square cushions as mattresses. These were called biscuits and invariably they slid apart before the night was over. Heat was provided by two small coal fired units. These units were about ten inches in diameter and about two feet tall. I think we were rationed to one coal bucket of coal per day. The building was about 50 feet long and about 20 wide. The floors were concrete, with concrete walls, both inside and out. Basically, they were nothing more than a shell. With the notorious cold, damp and foggy weather of England, it made for a pretty miserable habitat to reside in. There was a door at each end with an alcove with a second door. This assured that no light would escape at night during blackouts. There was one electric line from one end of the building to the other with single light bulbs hanging down about one foot. There were about five of these bulbs for the entire building. I noticed a number of pieces of paper twisted up though the roof around each of these bulbs. On questioning the veterans of the building I was told that if someone wanted the lights out they would yell turn off the lights and if this wasn't done, they would pull out their 45 caliber automatics and shot the bulbs out.

We soon learned where the mess hall, PX and all the other necessary buildings were. These buildings were all scattered and one had to do a lot of walking. Bicycles were prevalent. The mess hall as was the shower was at least a half mile. Warm water at the showers was provided only a couple of hours a day. Mostly, showers were with cold water.

**Ed Scamahorn**, at North Pickenham:

It seems to be a typical English Air Force base. Everything is housed in a Nissen hut type of building, the mess hall, PX, post office etc. We have two other crews (officer personnel) in the same hut with us. The enlisted crewmen share another hut with other enlisted crewmen just a short distance away.

**John Rex**, whose base was at Roudham Road, East Harling:

The base was typical construction for then: corrugated metal Quonset huts of several sizes used for shops, parts storage, mess hall, offices and so forth. And a rather flimsy looking metal bar building covered with a pressed paper material. However, they were more than adequate for the job since on a trip back to Roudham road in 1978 most of the buildings were still standing more than thirty five years after being built. Heat was provided by a simple metal can type stove that burned a soft smoky coal and was located in the centre of the building. The hut size was sufficient to house fifty to sixty

*Above and below:* Two impressions of a hut interior (cartoon by Jack Preston).

men. There were windows on both sides and at each end, the doors were at each end. Water for the base was stored in a two story square steel tank. The living area was separated from the technical area by about a mile.

**Roland Sabourin** (389 BG) wrote:

I don't recall ever feeling nice and comfortable at Wendling. I can remember trying to sleep over there when the pot-bellied stoves would go out. I had a couple electric heaters under my bed that I used to turn on at night trying to keep warm. That was somewhat successful. Basically it was always a chore to try and stay warm.

**Alfred Neumunz:**

We live in a small shack that is overcrowded. The rain leaks through the roof, the beds are hard like stone. Bicycles are the main mode of transportation, that is except for feet. We walk or ride miles to reach anything including bathroom facilities. Thus the musty odor of the barracks gives the impression of a pig pen … Today because of the extreme dampness everyone congregated around the hut's stove and tried to keep warm. That failing to do much good we started on some spirits and before long everyone was feeling mellow and life was worth living again. Someone stole six chickens and we all had southern fried which sort of sobered us up.

**Rudolph Howell:**

The rafters and other supports are made of wood, and the roof is made of steel (or tin, if you prefer). The floor is covered with linoleum that has seen more than its share of the war, and has great holes worn in it. I think that about covers the barracks as a whole. The particular room that we have has two double-decker bunks. It is a bit larger than the room we have just left. We now have two dressers and two lights. We have a very small coal stove, and the fellows that were here before us left us an oversize coal bin. I like this room because it's large.

For mattresses we have three 'biscuits' which are just cotton stuffed mattresses or pillows about two feet wide and long and about two inches thick. You lay three of them together and they invariably are too long for the bed. For a pillow we have a cylindrical filled pillow about 18 inches long and about five inches in diameter. For bedclothes we have blankets. There is no lack of blankets, but there's nothing else. I have one blanket wrapped over my mattress and pillow for my bottom 'sheet' and I have three more spread over for a top 'sheet' and cover. They are British blankets, and definitely inferior to ours.

**Jim McCrery:**

The English beds didn't have mattresses they had biscuits, something like three sofa cushions over the bed wires. It was difficult to wrap them together tight enough so they'd not separate and let your butt slip through a crack and rest on the wires which was cold and uncomfortable. Once successfully made, it was a wise man who left well alone; reason enough for infrequent sheet changes.

## Bicycles

**Rudolph Howell:**

Everyone (and I mean *everyone*) rides bicycles. If their destination is within four or five miles they walk. Lots of times some of the fellows offer to walk a girl home from a dance or somewhere, after she has said that she lives 'over the hill'. That turns out to be five or six miles down the road that generally cures them of walking the girls home ... I think I'll get myself a bicycle as soon as I get paid and can find one. They cost anywhere from six to ten pounds (so I understand) and a pound is worth approximately four dollars. I hope I can find one.

**Roy 'Jon' Jonasson** (389 BG):

This bike certainly comes in handy going to chow as it is over a mile to the mess hall and back and then when we wish to go to the PX or the show or up for our mail and so many things it saves so many steps. Yes, even now in the winter when it is cold, wet, muddy and rainy.

**Phillip Day:** 'I bought a bicycle about this time, a typical English model with hard, small diameter tires and calliper brakes on front and back wheels. I believe I paid four pounds ($16) for it.'

## Diet

All soldiers complain about their food, very often with good reason. For **John M. Rhoads** (389 BG), it was the continual appearance of one item of diet that annoyed him: '*Spam* – our cooks served it in various ways. For breakfast it may be mixed with powdered eggs. It has been served as a side dish with French toast and watery syrup ad nauseam.' He quoted a poem from The *Stars and Stripes* on the subject, part of which reads:

> All armies on their stomachs move, and this one moves on Spam,
> For breakfast they will fry it, for supper it is baked.
> For dinner it goes delicate – they have it pat-a-caked.

Plenty of other men had their own comments to make on the food:
    **Calvin Hanlyn:** 'The chow is the world's worst.'

*Right and below:* The bicycle was an essential
part of the airman's equipment.

**John van Acker:** 'We can't expect anything fancy here because we eat field rations. It is cheaper for us that way as the 21 dollars a month for food allotted to us covers it. Don't get me wrong – we get plenty to eat; it just isn't fancy.'
**Robert Doyle** (489 BG):

Once in a while one of us gets some rolls or something from a bakery, but usually they are dry, and not too exciting unless we had some jelly or something. My point is that if you could send some preserves, or something on that order, I could occasionally have a little snack. Also candy, or cookies, or both, enclosed with the jelly would be appreciated… I still have some cookies left, but they won't keep much longer because I'm here to eat them now. I'm munching some now. Very good! Superb! Thanks.

Incidentally, I am hungry about 100% of the time, so if you get a chance a package of goodies should be sent to me … Hershey bars or Milky Way bars etc. Milky Ways are very good when we take them up with us. Remember how we used to freeze them in the refrigerator. Well, we get the same effect here.

Kitchen duties

**Bill Horn** 437th Signal Construction Battalion: 'On K.P. [Kitchen Patrol, known also as Kitchen Police] from 5:30 a.m. to 6:15 p.m. Tough day behind the dishwashing machine.'

**Ed Scamahorn:** 'Wonder of wonders, we had ice cream for our evening meal. This is the first time I have had any in months. They had contrived to send up an airplane on a test flight to 24,000 feet and made the ice cream up there where it was way below freezing.'

**Charles Barlow:** 'We have to get ration points to get cigarettes, soap, matches and soap & can only get a very limited amount of each. We can get plenty of cigarettes but matches are very scarce. If you happen to run across a lighter that you can light in the wind, I'd sure like to have it.'

**Robert Boyle,** 3 June 1944: 'Alice, if at any time you get any candy, or cookies, or fruit juice or the like that you can send, please do. I realize that some things are hard to get over in the States too, so don't use your ration cards for them.'

**Clayton Wiseman:** 'Missed Dinner but was glad as the stew was poor. Ate enough for three at supper. Got two packages from home and it is perfect. The candy did not last long, but that is expected. Just like Xmas opening them.'

**John van Acker,** 28 March 1945:

This morning I had two eggs – fresh eggs for breakfast! Sounds commonplace doesn't it! But over here it is one of the rarest of treats. Us fellows in the army are lucky because we get served real eggs once or twice a month. The common Englishman is lucky if he had a dozen eggs since the war started – over five years ago! And believe me after trying to stomach those powdered eggs a few weeks one really appreciates a fresh egg when

The airman's diet (John van Acker).

he gets one. It literally melts in your mouth. I sure would like some milk too but that is really out of the question. Haven't had a glass of cold, rich milk since November.

**Vyto Enovitch:** 'Before briefing I filled myself with four luscious fresh fried eggs, sunny side up. That was more than I've eaten for a long time.'
   **Paul Steichen:**

We got ahold of two fresh eggs this morning and the co-pilot is now cooking them (hard-boiling). I've had a total of three fresh eggs since I got off the boat. That and milk is the only food I've missed, having had no milk. Otherwise I think our food is very good. If you ever send another package and have any room in it you could put in a few hard-boiled eggs. It's a big propaganda stunt that we get fresh eggs before every mission but it's just a big lie. Tonight we heard a broadcast to the states and it made mention of the flyboys getting fresh eggs. That makes me mad.

**John Rhoads** explained the PX system, incidentally revealing the natural generosity of these young Americans:

All Yanks carried a PX ration card. We were permitted to draw each week only a certain amount of rationed items, including tobacco products, candy, gum and soap. Candy and chewing gum were favorites among the children … A box was left inside the PX door at the airfield for us to drop bars of candy and blocks of gum into. These were distributed to needy children.

Rhoads also noted that at first it was only privates and corporals who did KP – he was annoyed when it was extended to include sergeants like him!

## Baths and Laundry

**Ed Scamahorn:** 'I cleaned up and turned in some clothes to the laundry and cleaning unit. It will take about nine days for either of these services and I am wondering if I can make the rest of my clothes last that long. (It actually took three weeks).'
   **Paul Steichen:** 'Sent my laundry out to some woman who does it in 3 days and it came back all wet, so I guess she gets no more of my business.'
   **Jim McCrery:**

Visiting lads from North Pickenham came onto the base to collect our soiled washables which their mothers would launder and fold and the boys would return. I think the mothers did it more as a gesture of kindness towards us for they charged us so little … For dry cleaning someone would scrounge a five gallon pail of 100 octane gas into which we would dip our woolens and hang them out to dry. The lead compounds would give the garments more body and the faint petrol aroma would give our flyer image a touch of realism.

**Bob Doyle:**

As far as me being able to take a bath here, we have showers. I take a bath occasionally. Laundry is handled by the army, as is dry cleaning, but it is very unreliable. I send my laundry to a lady who lives near here, and my cleaning I take into the small town near here. It takes care of my requirements.

Oh yes, speaking of clothes, you needn't worry about any long drawers for me. I think I can get some from the army quartermaster store in London. Beside the two pair I have is sufficient, as I only use them for flying now.

**Roland Sabourin** at Wendling: 'Down next to the officers' club was a shower set-up. An outdoor shower where you could go every couple of days and clean up. The water was warm but the shower was outside. It was a sort of test of your individual strength to take a shower in that thing. It was a survival affair.'

**Alfred Neumunz:** 'We've all stocked in much woollies and clothing. The mornings are killing – getting up into a damp cold, each one I say is the end – How we suffer for democracy??!'

**John van Acker:**

We are slowly getting settled in our little hut. Clothes hangars [*sic*] had to be made and we made some little bedside tables, with shelves inside, out of bomb cases. Fortunately we have a bureau between three of us.

We even have electricity but they are pretty stingy with it over here and turn it off sometimes. The British use 230 Volts so I haven't been able to use my razor yet. If I ever get to a town I am going to get a transformer.

## Animals

There were animals on the bases, some more welcome than others, as recalled by **Roy Jonasson:** 'When I was in town the other day I bought a couple of mouse traps and managed to get some of those mice that run over my blankets and go hunting for food. During the night I heard the trap snap at the foot of my bed and sure enough I had him. The rats over here are really big.'

**Ed Kelly** (445 BG) claimed that the mice in his Old Buckenham barracks were so big that he woke up one evening and saw them carrying his Christmas packages out of the back door! He recalled:

Out here in the area we have a black, white and brown spotted dog with fuzzy hair, an airdale [*sic*] head and as smart as a whip. We have lots of fun with him. He is entirely a GI dog and is friendly only to a GI and not to the British Civilian workers on the base. You see he knows where his dinner comes from! He enjoys running after rabbits in the woods just outside the door and likes for us to go with him. We do have so much fun with him and he is a real chow hound, as we are. Yes, he also refuses some of the food we do not like.

Cows and planes, Rackheath.

## Lack of Privacy

The huts did not lend themselves to those who wanted a period of quiet.

**Ken Jones:** 'The togetherness of the military life became almost overwhelming at times. You slept in a crowd, trained in a group, ate together, shaved and showered together. There were few opportunities for privacy.'

**Rudolph Howell:** 'I figured with Parsons gone there would be no one to come in and disturb me so I could write all I wanted to and as long as I wanted to. But sure as I started writing a character came in and started shooting the breeze and apparently he intends to stop here all night so I don't know how much I will be able to write.'

On another occasion, **Howell** wrote: 'I just can't write when someone is talking and people are always in here talking. They talk about everything in the world from the local customs in Arcadia, Flak, to the number of prisoners captured by Montgomery yesterday.'

## Air Raids

By the time the Americans arrived, the worst air attacks by Germany on Norfolk were over, but there were still occasional air raids.

**Ray Waters** (448 BG):

April 11 1944: Germans bombed our field today but dropped only seven bombs.

April 18 1944: The Jerrys again bombed very near here. The explosions shook the barracks. Later they strafed our field with machine gun or cannon fire. One fellow found a hole through his bed when he returned from the air raid shelter.

On 22 April 1944, aircraft from eleven Bomb Groups were returning later than was usual from bombing missions to Germany. The airfield lights acted as beacons and their stream was infiltrated by German fighter aircraft who had followed them home on what became known as the 'Night of the Intruders'.

**Ray Waters** recorded events at **Seething**:

April 22 1944: our planes went to Hamm Germany today. They didn't take off until in the afternoon so they were late returning. In fact it was after 10 o'clock. The Germans followed them and when they turn[ed] their lights on to land the Jerrys would shoot them down. I saw about six bombers go down burning and one German fighter. The sky was the same as the fair on fireworks night. Burning planes, tracer flares, and flak. We lost six planes.

We didn't know that German Me410 night fighters had followed us back to England because it was full dark and they were apparently using clouds as cover. However, the English anti-aircraft batteries knew they were there because they showed up on radar. So a situation developed where English anti-aircraft batteries were firing at the

German fighters who were firing at the American bombers who were firing at the German fighters. It was mass confusion on the grand scale, and no one could say who caused damage to which planes.

The first plane to attempt to land at Seething was Liberator 42-94744 of the 714th Bomb Squadron. Following standard procedure 42-94744 turned on its landing lights as it approached Seething, which was the signal for Seething tower to turn on the runway lights. With its landing lights on the plane made an excellent target and the German fighters simply followed the runway lights, and fired at a point between the two landing lights of the plane. The bomber's starboard engine was set afire forcing the pilot to pull up so the crew could bail out, and the bomber crashed at Worlingham just beyond Seething.

The second plane to come in was the 'Vadie Ray' and she was on fire. Most of the crew had bailed out but the pilots, Skaggs and Blum, brought the plane down on the main runway, then swerved it off the runway and into the field so it wouldn't block the landing of the following planes. The remainder of the crew got out and ran to safety just before the 'Vadie Ray' exploded. The explosion and fire produced dense smoke which blew across and greatly reduced visibility on the main runway.

The third plane to come in landed safely, but was strafed as it rolled up the runway. The crew got the plane to the end of the runway, but because of the strafing they abandoned it there and ran for the safety of a revetment. Our plane, 'Ice Cold Katie', was the fourth plane to land and as we came in on our final approach we could see the smoke from the 'Vadie Ray' but, because of the smoke, we couldn't see the plane stopped at the end of the runway. We experienced some strafing as we rolled up the runway, and it wasn't until we passed through the smoke from 'Vadie Ray' that we were able to see the plane blocking the runway ahead. The pilots were able to stop 'Ice Cold Katie' just short of that plane and, because of the strafing, we left the plane and ran for the relative safety of a revetment.

The fifth plane to come in got down safely but as it passed through the smoke from 'Vadie Ray' it found two planes blocking the end of the runway and was not able to stop before slamming into the tail of 'Ice Cold Katie' forcing it into the plane in front. When the pile-up stopped the crew of this plane jumped out and ran for the revetment. One of the gunners somehow caught his parachute on something as he jumped out of the waist window and the ripcord was pulled. In the midst of the disaster and strafing we all had to laugh as we watched him run for safety with his parachute pulling out behind him. Now there were three planes blocking the end of the main runway and one on fire beside it, so the rest of the Group had to land on the short runway.

The strafing continued for what seemed like a long time, but it must have been just minutes, then the German fighters were gone from Seething.

Bombs were also dropped on **Rackheath** airbase. One of the ground crew, **Allen Welters**, recalled what happened. He had been working late on a B-24, had a 'quick chow', and then called in to his Squadron's Engineering hut to see if any late duties had been assigned:

As I entered my area I was surprised to find the whole area deserted, no one was around which was unusual indeed! Upon entering the Squadron Engineering hut I found no one there, and then I saw the weapons rack was unlocked, and all the weapons were gone except mine, and mine had a note on it! The note was for me, and it said to take my weapon and head for the woods behind the Bomb-Dump, where the rest of my Squadron's ground personnel was supposed to be, 'looking for saboteurs' that have been seen in that area.

I headed for the dump with my weapon. This was in the same direction as the north end of our runway. Darkness was setting in, and as I neared the bomb dump I picked up the sound of what seemed to be a strange aircraft o– something just did not set right, and a strange feeling came over me, a feeling that nothing good was about to happen. I stopped and listened more closely, when all of a sudden I heard a twin-engined aircraft approaching over the tree tops, as I thought this might be a German plane!

Welters did not fire, however, as he thought the plane could possibly be British:

Then the gun pit and the south end of the field began firing at an aircraft as it was heading south, the tracers following it! … A hellish battle occurred, with planes flying in all directions, tracers between the aircraft, and anti-aircraft fire. It is then that I saw a B-24 flame up and go down behind the woods, then another B-24 burst into flames and went down. Just standing there I realized how much those crews were fighting go out of hell they were in and be able to see where to land. 'God help them down' I prayed. Just as suddenly the battle ended and ones of our planes landed.

In total, fourteen aircraft were shot down on that night. The German attack killed a member of the ground crew at Rackheath, Private **Daniel E. Miney**. **Allen Welters** recalled that Miney was a Quartermaster. He had told Welters that he knew very little of what actually went on at the base, so Welters had invited him to come along on his night off and have a look. Unfortunately his night off was that of 22 April and he was caught up in the attack, with fatal results.

Miney is the only member of a ground crew listed on the 2nd Air Division's Roll of Honor as killed in action. Of course, several other members of the ground crews and support staff died in accidents. The most notable was on 15 July 1944: at 7.30 p.m. the bomb dump at Metfield blew up, detonating over 1000 tons of bombs and explosives, killing five or six men, wrecking five B-24 bombers and severely damaging several more. The blast could be heard forty miles away. The men killed were not from the base but from a truck company unit based at Earsham. They included three men whose names are recorded on the wall of the missing at Madingley, Donald Adkins, Donald Hurley and Steve Suchey.

Conditions improved on the bases as the item passed – or the men became more accustomed to them.

**Calvin Hanlyn:**

The weather is so bad we can't fly. The fog has closed in to a level of about four inches and it hasn't stopped raining for a week. We finally have our own mess hall and the food has improved until now it is just England's worst. They finally installed electric lights but they are so dim we still have to light matches to walk from one end of the barracks to the other.

**Robert Boyle,** 10 July 1944: 'Things here are about the same. Flying, eating and sleeping. Some of the 'bugs' are being worked out, and we are getting more organized in certain items, such as passes.'

**Roy Jonasson**: 'The base would remind you of a main street down town on a Saturday night, only all work. All kinds of lights were burning and the colored lights on the Fuel trucks and trailors [*sic*], and the various colored lights on our planes as they come in and taxi about, and the lights of the vehicles.'

# Chapter Six

# The Support Staff

The pilots were quick to appreciate the work of the support staff or ground crew on the bases.

**Calvin Hanlyn:**

> Another week has gone by and we have made three attempts to fly. Each time the weather closes in and we have to return to base. Almost every day we are up at 0400 and after eating dash down to the briefing room. Out to the planes and just before take off the mission is scrubbed. Sometimes we take off and just as we are leaving the coast we get a recall. Then all the bombs have to be unloaded, guns have to be pulled and cleaned. Those poor armament men spend all their time loading and unloading bombs. And believe me, that's hard work.

**Frederick Porter:** 'The most difficult bombs to load were the 20-pound fragmentation bombs ... Each bomb was fitted with a light gage sheet metal fin which cut up the hands of the people handling them.'

**John C. Rowe** (48 BG): 'From the nose to the tail, mechanics and ordnance men were truly members of the combat crew and not just "ground crews."'

They were innovative, hard-nosed men patching up and loading the 'birds' to keep the flight crews in the air. Without their dedication and around-the-clock hours in rains, snow, sleet, wind and fog, the flight crews would never have gotten off the ground.

On another occasion, Rowe wrote:

> Ground crews treated the planes under their responsibility as they would their children. They worked in bitter cold, rain, wind and snow. Many built eight foot high shelters on the front line from old 'bomb crates'. They 'sweated out' each returning mission and were on hand to see the flight crews come in. They were always exceedingly interested in 'their' planes, how they performed and what was needed to keep them in the best possible condition.

Diaries and letters by support staff are less common than those of aircrew, but they have a lot to say about their daily lives. First, the airbases had to be built.

Working on a plane: the two men at the engine are Joe Miele and Lee Quesnell; Joe Tangorra is in front.

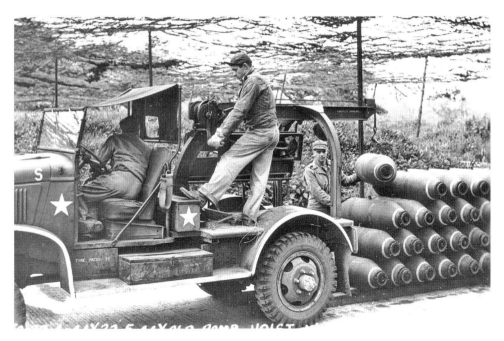

Loading bombs, Shipdham.

The work was done by men like **Bill Horn**:

25 Nov 1942: started work on an 800 poleline job. This line is to be used for a lighting system around Shipdham airdrome, which was our old, first station in England. Went to the field by truck [from Hethel where he was based]. And dug 28 holes 4½ feet deep, and set 6 poles. A good day's work: feeling tired tonight.

Thanksgiving Day: Up at 5:30 a.m. Hauled and set poles [at Shipdham] until 4:15 p.m. Went to Norwich this evening and saw vaudeville show at Hippodrome theatre. Had 2 fine meals today; one at Shipdham where we are working and one at Hethel when we returned. *But*, no turkey this Thanksgiving. Job coming along good. Hard work.

The work continued on the following day, but then:

28 Nov: Dug pole lines all day. Job slowed up due to some mistake in the laying out of the line. Many holes that were dug cannot be used; a lot of hard, wasted labor. This poleline is about 12 miles long and circles the airdrome. It must be layed [*sic*] out accurately because of plane landings. Poles set 180–200 yards apart.

29 Nov: Got a break this Sunday; no work, as sergeants are taking some sort of a test. Wrote letters, shined shoes, and did a bit of sewing. Got one more tetanus shot this afternoon. Taking it easy tonight. Catching up on my reading. Heard PM Churchill's speech on the air tonight.

1 Dec: Back on the job (at Shipdham); put up and served (dressed) guy wires. Felt

good to climb again. One of our trucks was hit on the way to work and one fellow was knocked unconscious: he is OK now.

Just a week later, Horn was on the move again:

Left Hethel at 9 p.m. and boarded train at Wymondham. Truck stuck in mud on way to station, had to wait for another. Rode on train all night, off at Aintree about 9 a.m. [on 9 December], rode to Liverpool dock in a street car (tram) and boarded the *Empress of Canada* around noon of Dec 9th. *Off To N. Africa*

Horn had been in Norfolk for just twenty days.

Extracts from the letters home of **Roy Jonasson** make a fine record of how the ground crews approached their work:

I am out here in the dispersal area again this Sunday evening and one would never dream that this was a Sunday or a Sunday evening with everything that is going on here.

But I am glad of all this activity as that will make that many more Sundays sooner that we will be able to spend together.

If you were here you would see propeller changes, engine change, super charger change and much other activity and you would see all this activity is going on so smoothly as if the boys were masters of it – and they really are efficient at it. There is no confusion; they are just like veterans.

As I rode my bicycle back from supper this evening many thoughts came to my mind as I passed by various spots – how good they looked, how the various mechanics were getting them ready for another mission. The boys are so proud of the planes they look after.

…

As I rode my bike out to the area early this morning I thought of you and what time it was in Denver. It was very dark except in the North and there it was showing a little light and one could see hundreds of stars twinkling in the inky sky. The cold wind blew in from the North as I went down the winding road which led to the Mess Hall on my way. I stopped to get a cup of coffee but the doors were still locked so I went on my way as the others did, as it was very early. Well, by the time I got out to the airplanes I was wide awake. Soon you could hear the familiar run-up of the engines that we used to hear in Denver, but much earlier. Trucks, jeeps, bicycles and various other forms of transportation and carriers were going about and soon our bombers were off again.

…

The news has been good the last few days and I am glad because our boys over on the Continent need help and we hope and pray the news continues to be good. I believe it will be.

…

At noon time the truck comes around the perimeter and picks up the men working on the line who do not have bicycles and takes them to chow. Well, we have a black goat

Ground crew beside plane, 'Old Buck' [Old Buckenham].

A well-earned break.

out there that we have raised and the other day the boys jumped in the truck and the goat ran up to it and wanted to get on. He bleated as the truck pulled away and ran after it but one of the mechanics on his bicycle pulled it back. The goat spends all of the time grazing and playing round the airplane. He sure is a pet.

…

Last night it rained hard all night and the wind blew but I had my heavy leather jacket and trousers on and my steel helmet which kept me dry except for my face. How I love to have the rain wash my face. Sometimes it feels good to be out in the rain. It gives a person a feeling all of its own, especially over here.

…

The poppies certainly are nice and bright red today. They stood out so clearly today in the green meadows. They remind me of what they would look like in Normandy as we are in [censored] country just [censored] from [censored]. Many of the buildings here have the Norman architecture, as one finds in Normandy, France. I imagine the wind has blown the seeds across the channel from that country.

…

We are now permitted to mention the rocket P-Planes. We are all safe and in no danger at the present time.

It is 11 p.m. and I am still out at the dispersal area and will stay here all night because in about two hours things will begin to stir again for another early mission.

…

Why I have had my breakfast and been out here on the line all day yesterday and all night but I'll get to go in about 8 a.m., after the planes take off on another mission.

…

I do feel good because my stomach is full of hotcakes and hot coffee, yes lots of them. They serve breakfast from five to eight a.m. and the early 'chow hounds' always get more hot cakes whereas later, from seven to eight, they dish them out to you.

…

We were pretty busy all day yesterday and last night up to 2 a.m. as we received some new planes that had to be modified, along with seven engine changes on some of our old planes.

…

If you were here now you would see a lovely sunset in the west. Our planes are coming in one by one, to their home after a mission. Yes, an occasional B 26, a P 47, a P 51 some of them do stop here. You would see the repairing of the runways and the perimeter on a big scale by an engineering unit (Negro). They really work fast with all their large modern equipment.

26 Dec 1944; Christmas morning I was up at 5:30 a.m. and was greeted by Pete shaking me and saying, 'Jon, there is a mission taking off at …' Well, I jumped out of my cot and landed on some newspapers in my bare feet. You see, I carefully place the newspapers beside my bed on the cold cement floor and it is not so cold. Well, I dressed, and before you can say 'Jack Robinson' too! When I stepped outside I was

greeted with a White Christmas of heavy frost. Ice had formed on the sprocket of my bicycle and chain but by shaking it loose I was able to pedal away to the mess hall some distance away. I had a dish of hot oatmeal, bread, and apple butter and hot coffee. Then I pedalled back to the line and went to work.

It was some sight to see the planes being warmed up, the ice and all, the crews working hard to clear it and the frost. The men were checking and rechecking. It reminded me of Santa reloading his sleigh with more cargo but of a different nature. But cargo to help bring this war to a close.

Well, our planes went off safely and returned with battle damage which was soon remedied by the ground crew.

I went on roving guard at 5:30 p.m. and was relieved at 10:30 p.m. So you see it was a busy day but I loved it because it was one more successful mission and that helped our boys that are doing the ground fighting.

For dinner we had turkey, potatoes, canned peas (and how I love canned peas, remember?), cranberry sauce, coffee, bread, butter and dressing with gravy.

This makes the third Christmas in the Army and may it be the last!!!! How thankful I am to know that we are over half way and that people all over the world will have peace within reasonable time.

An unknown member of the 789th Squadron ground personnel at Rackheath gave an excellent description of what the ground crew actually did, recollecting especially the *noises*:

They found the sky was the roof overhead and the huge open field was the space for their A/C [aircraft] repair and maintenance stalls. They performed their technical duties in any kind of the bad weathers, on frost covered wings and engine cowls, on cold and greasey [sic] engine parts that required to be done bare handed. Much of the work on the A/C had to be performed at night when most times a flash lite was the only lite – if the batteries were available... To stop and listen to all the noises on the line at the hours of midnite and after was unbelievable, the chatter of the sheet-metal men, auxiliary motors whine in aiding powers for the different repairs that had to be done, men shuffling about in different efforts in the darkness to accomplish their tasks, rattle of cowling, the laboring noises of the ordinance trucks and men loading the tons of bombs, the Commo men working on the radios, men struggling with the many belts of ammo, the instrument, electricians and prop men serious about their precise work to be done, the rulers struggling with the long fuel hoses to the top of the wings and the screeching noise of reeling in hoses. The missions for the Aircrews usually were for early take-offs so the ground crews had to be on duties anywhere from 0230 hrs on. While their A/C [aircraft] were on their missions the Crew Chiefs and mechanics were not at ease as they were thinking and hoping their A/C were performing well and that there would not be a failure to be the cause for the aircrews to lose their lives. At the time of the return of the A/C was the time you could see the sign of anxiety or happiness on their faces.

852nd Bomb Squadron, Armament Section.

Loading extra fuel.

The Machine Shop, Halesworth.

**James Caulfield** was another member of the support staff:

I was among the ground echelon picked to go to North Pickenham to operate the new base. I was a teletype operator at Base HQ and in the 856th Bomb Squadron. We were at North Pickenham from 11th March to the 11th August 1944, our barrack site was on a hill side near the Swaffham–Thetford LNER tracks. We would go down the hill and turn right to the Mess Hall, going up the hill a way and to the left were the runways and the HQ center. We had our bikes and went to various towns in all directions.

**James Chew:**

As I had been a Control Tower Operator back in the States, I was given the Special Duty job as Airfield Controller. The Van I occupied had a fiberglass dome, where I had 360-degree visibility, and could see all the runways of the Airdrome. I had red and green signal lamps, and a Very pistol I could use that fired red flares in the event of dire emergency. An underground telephone line was terminated at the end of each runway, so that I could be in constant touch with Operations in the Control Building.

## Black Personnel

Men at the airbases included some who were themselves emigrants from Europe to the States, such as Ludwig Lund from Denmark, and many children of immigrants such as

The control tower

Leo Ruvolis, the son of a coal miner from Lithuania, and Harold Kren, whose family was from Hungary. They included some whose families had come from Germany. This could create tensions within the heart of a man such as **Ken Jones:**

> My mixed ancestry of Welch–German puts me in the third generation removed from original German potato water soup, *hassenpheler* and flour sack bloomers. There is a certain kind of kinship with the old country. I never heard a flyer speak of hating Germans. We disliked Nazis with a passion but this did not include the German people. There was a fine distinction that all Germans were not alike. We never flew in anger or hatred.

The diversity of origin of the men on the bases reflected the history of the United States. They included Mexican-Americans and Native Americans. Ben Kuroki, who served on thirty missions in the European Theatre, was a Japanese-American, later becoming the only Japanese-American to serve in the Pacific Theatre. One group was originally not represented among the 'friendly invaders'. At the beginning of the war there were no African-Americans in the Air Force. In 1942, it was ordered to accept blacks at a rate of 10 per cent of its total force. Black fighter pilots began to be trained in the States, but in East Anglia African-Americans did not serve as pilots but with segregated ordinance, quartermaster and transportation companies. These units were under the umbrella title of 'Combat Support Wing' from August 1943.

Black personnel in 'Wings for Victory' parade.

Segregation was also practised in leisure time. Certain pubs and dance halls might be restricted to one race only, or passes might be given to particular groups on particular days, in effect establishing separate 'Black' and 'White' nights. Even the American Red Cross in practise had separate clubs for black GI's, such as that at Bungay. Whole towns might also be assigned as places specifically for black personnel. One of the few memoirs to discuss this was that of **James Chew:**

> There was not one black man in our whole group. Nor were there any Blacks in any other Bomber or Fighter Group. Black GI's were generally assigned to Quartermaster Outfits in those days, and they stayed very much to themselves – usually near a small town. There was one at Bungay, somewhere between Halesworth and Norwich. Those men never went outside Bungay. Likewise, no white men ventured into Bungay.

Black GI's knew they couldn't go into any other Cities or Towns, as white GI's had already become established there. It would have been sheer folly as well as dangerous for them to do so. They had to stay in the Town close by their Quartermaster Group, or whatever type of Base they were operating.

The author Martin W. Bowman notes that the Duke of Connaught on Prince of Wales Road in Norwich was a popular haunt of the black Americans.

Just one case of racial abuse is recorded in the Second Air Division Memorial Library archives: a private in 491 BG was charged with using the 'N' word to the soldiers of Company B, 827th Engineer (Aviation) Battalion at Metfield on the night of 17 June 1944. The man was court-martialled and fined $40 with three months hard labour, but the confinement was suspended.

The international nature of war brought new experiences for many men. Two examples both relate to popular music:

**Rudolph Howell:** 'The sergeant in the next room has a radio and I just heard an Englishman singing a negro spiritual. Now that was really sharp. A negro dialect with a British accent. It was the first time that I had ever heard of that and I got quite a kick out of it.'

**Roy Jonasson:**

Dearest, so many times I think of you and wish you were along with me. Then I think that one of these days you will be with me. And what a grand day that will be. You see, dearest, you are my 'Lilli Marlene'. That was the name of the picture I saw here yesterday. It is a song written by a German soldier about his sweetheart he left back home. This song has taken all of the soldiers by storm, especially all of us that are away from our sweethearts. You see, we all have Lilli Marlenes, too, and you are the best Lilli of them all to me. There is a record by the same name and we listen to it many times. This song was first sung over the radio by a Swedish singer by the name of Lilli Larson and it made a hit from then on to all soldiers on both sides. Hear the record if you can.

## Women Personnel

People in Norfolk remember the American airmen but do not often mention a vital part of the war effort: the contribution of American women.

The Women's Army Auxiliary Corps (WAAC) was formed in May 1942 as a women's auxiliary unit in the United States Army. It later became the Women's Army Corps (WAC), from 1943, when it was converted from auxiliary to full status. During the Second World War, around 150,000 American women served in the WAAC and WAC. Initially the WACs, as the first women other than nurses to serve in the United States Army, met some opposition from both within the Army and conservative public opinion. However, many Generals were soon requesting more WACs and one General in the United States Army, Douglas MacArthur, called them 'my best soldiers'.

The Air Force was especially anxious to obtain WACs. Eventually it obtained 40 per cent of all WACs in the Army. In July 1943, the first battalion of WACs to reach the European Theatre of Operations arrived in London. These 557 enlisted women and nineteen officers were assigned to duty with the 8th Air Force. A second battalion of WACs, earmarked for the 8th Air Force, reached London between 20 September 1943 and 18 October 1943. The majority of these women worked as telephone switchboard operators, clerks, typists, secretaries, and motor pool drivers. In general, WACs in the ETO held a limited range of job assignments: 35 per cent worked as stenographers and typists, 26 per cent were clerks, and 22 per cent were in communications work. Only 8 per cent were assigned jobs considered unusual for women: mechanics, draftsmen,

WACs at work and play. *Below*: The back of the Ginnery photograph gives the names (left to right): William Blume, Hazel Bliss, Virginia Bowdoin, Maurice Layfield, Evelyn Cohen, Doris Ogden. Evelyn is also third from the left in the upper picture.

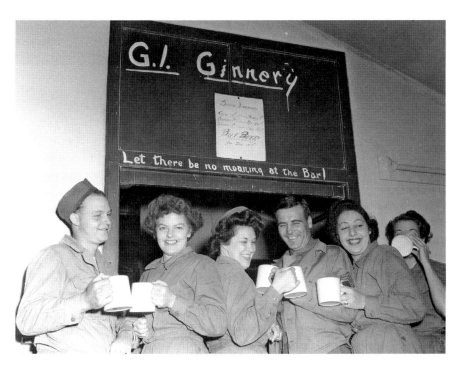

WACs and airmen make the base their home.

interpreters, and weather observers. However, they performed vital work in their own right, and also freed up men for front-line duties. They worked at headquarters and also on the bases themselves. At any one time during 1943–1945, there were about 200 American servicewomen in Norfolk. The programme for a WAC basketball event in January 1945 summed up their achievement:

> Today, the third anniversary of the 8th Air Force, we are commemorating the activation of a military force which has grown from a courageous experiment to a powerful team – that team is making a substantial contribution to the inevitable victory of the allies. No small part of our growth and achievements can be attributed to the success of the Women's Army Corps, who have served with ever-increasing effectiveness with the 8th Air Force since July 1943. The spirit, the team-work and the aggressiveness which members of the WAC of the 8th Air Force display in organised athletics is symbolic of the way in which they acquit their military responsibilities. When the final history of this command is written, theirs will be a glowing chapter.

## Nurses

Other women served in a more traditional role – as nurses. The Station Hospital was at Morley Hall, near Wymondham. The hospital was not segregated, serving all men on the airbases. The buildings have since become Wymondham College. It is said that the spirit of an airman from nearby Hethel who died there still walks at night between the hospital and the base. In anticipation of casualties from the D-Day landings, the hospital was ordered to increase its capacity from about 834 to 1,254 beds. On 12 July 1944, medical supply personnel prepared 200 stretchers in two hours ready for the first mass admission of these battle casualties from a hospital train at Wymondham Station. Eight hospital trainloads, 2099 patients, were admitted.

**Roy Jonasson** saw them arrive:

last night another fellow, Russel Sciandra and I went for a ride on our bicycles to the little village of Wymondham where they were having an American ball game between our team and a team from another base. After the game we rode by the railroad station and saw them unload wounded American soldiers from a hospital train, a sight I shall never forget. We are all so lucky to be at our work and certainly have so much to be thankful for.

## The Official Artist

The 2nd Air Division even had an official war artist, Ludwig Lund. Lund was born in Odense, Denmark, in 1908. He and his family emigrated to the United States in 1920, when Lund was twelve. He served in the United States Army Air Force and was named the Official Illustrator of the 2nd Air Division. He painted both scenes of air force activity and also pictures of Norwich and of the English countryside. A collection of his paintings was presented to General Hodges in December 1943, while others were sent back to his wife Phyllis and are now in the possession of his daughter, Marjorie Lund-Fontaine. He later wrote: 'While I was stationed in England during World War Two, I found the inspiration I was sympathetic to. Everywhere I turned I found pictures to be painted. It was the European in me. It was as if I had found something I had lost long ago.'

Several of the other airmen drew sketches or cartoons illustrating their life in England, and three of them are represented in this book: **John Van Acker** (491 BG), **Jack M. Preston** (467 BG) and **Ray Waters** (448 BG).

# Chapter Seven

# Entertainment

Americans, of course, have their own celebrations – Fourth of July and Thanksgiving. At Old Buckenham, on one occasion the young airmen celebrated the Fourth of July by setting off flares and by shooting out the light bulbs in the barracks with their pistols! The Squadron Commander did not approve!

At the very least a special meal could be expected. Commanding Officer, Eugene Snavely, and officers of the 44th Bomb Group, sat down to a Thanksgiving meal. Their menu included tomato juice, roast turkey with a sage dressing, cranberry jelly, snowflake potatoes with giblet gravy, candied sweet potatoes, buttered peas, pumpkin pie with sliced cheese, and fresh fruit and candy for desert.

Men might find entertainment within their huts.

**Roy Jonasson**: 'We are having a grand time here in the barrack this evening. It is raining heavily outside but here Mike is playing with his mouth organ. And the rest of us are singing songs from a book that Bill Wood (the organist at Denver) has. In another corner a chess game is going on.'

**James Chew**, at Halesworth:

On payday, which was the last day of the month, a lot of the guys would gather around someone's bunk and play poker. Sometimes I would stop and watch them play, never indulging, myself. Zim would always look up at me and ask: 'Wanta learn the game, Dave?' I would smile, shaking my head negatively. Then I would ask, 'How do you guys figure out how to play your cards?' He would smile, saying, 'You gotta know when to hold 'em – know when to fold 'em – and know when to walk away'. I knew Zim was an old gambler, and that his advice was the voice of wisdom.

There were many other forms of entertainment on the bases, whether relaxing over a beer or watching a film or show. Some entertainers travelled the bases in support of the troops, such as the actor James Cagney.

**Clayton Wiseman**: '28 March: USO Show tonight. We went to the show at 4.30 and it did not start until 6.30. James Cagney was the main attraction but the others stole the show especially Al Bernie. The show was worth sweating out two hours.'

**Paul Steichen**: 'Since I've been here I've only been in town [Norwich] once and that was in the afternoon from 2–5. We can go in every nite but I just don't have any desire

James Cagney entertains the troops.

to. All there is in there is shows, beer and women. We have the former two on the field and naturally the latter isn't interesting me.'

**Rudolph Howell:**

I have just returned from the show where I saw Betty Grable in *Pin Up Girl*. It was the second time I had seen it but that didn't phase [*sic*] me at all. I go every time the picture changes. It's about all there is to do around here for entertainment. Besides, I wanted to go and see our new theater. It just opened last night and I didn't go. I think it is supposed to be one of the nicest ones around here anyway.

**John Rhoads:**

The officers and non-commissioned officers (Staff Sergeant and above) had their individual clubs and the lower ranking enlisted men – Private through Sergeant (three stripers) had to use the NAAFI club. However, officers and NCOs came to the NAAFI club often. Operated by volunteers from the British community, the NAAFI club served non-carbonated soft drinks, hot tea and tea cakes (crumpets). Serving alcoholic beverages was permitted at the Officer and NCO clubs but was not permitted at the NAAFI ... Later the American Red Cross took over from the NAAFI and the club's

American airmen and Land Army girls socialize at Shipdham.

name was changed to Aero Club ... The extended facilities included a well-equipped library, a writing room, a game room and a music room. A variety of records were placed in the music room for our enjoyment.

# Sport

Many of the young men and women on the bases enjoyed sports, especially those that they were used to, including basketball, baseball and boxing.
**Mary Williams-Elder:**

Well, you can congratulate us – we just won the 8th Air Force Basketball Championship for WACs. We went on a little trip last Saturday – played 1st Division Sunday afternoon and beat them 37–14, and then that night we played 8th AF HQ for the Championship and beat them 37–18. Puch, the first sergeant (pronounced Puck) came out of the game with a beautiful shiner. It really is a peach. I got a jammed finger and a bruised knee, but otherwise I'm fine. Embry got the same thing but she is

*Above and next page:* Sporting successes: 491 BG touch football winners; programme for Eighth Air Force Ladies' Basketball contest, 28 January 1945.

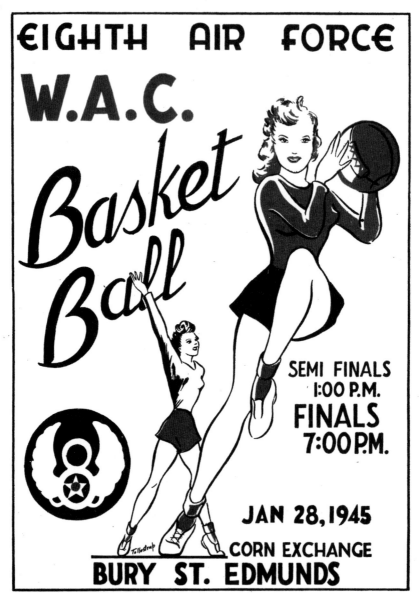

FREER & HAYTER, PRINTERS, HIGH WYCOMBE

OK today. Went to a dance last night, and every time anyone would bump into me I was in agony – not really, but it did hurt. I was stiff and sore in every joint. They (the team) all laughed at me because I didn't fall down but once in the first game, and was bragging about it – but the second game – oh my – I played most of it on the floor. What a beating I took, but I lived thru it. It was well worth while.

Sometimes local people could watch these events, such as the 'rodeo' held on Norwich City Football Ground.
**Roy Jonasson,** 6 August 1944:

At 6:30 p.m. I went to the rodeo put on by the American soldiers. All money raised went to the war charities of England. I have enclosed a clipping from the newspaper telling of the 'Flying Cowboys'. First, these boys did their duties, both combat and ground men, and then they put on this rodeo show. The English people really enjoyed it and it was the first time some of them had ever seen anything like it.

Boxing was helped by the presence among the men of the legendary Billy Conn, who sometimes took part in exhibition bouts. Joe Louis, the 'Black Bomber' was also in Norfolk on a number of occasions.
Cricket was a strange English game that some American airmen were willing to try.
**Frederick Porter:**

While in the Air Force I spent some time in Merry Ol' England. Now the English are fine folk but they do some things and say some things that are mighty strange to us. They drive on the wrong side of the road, drink warm beer, and call the hood of a car the bonnet, the trunk the boot, and hold their pants up with braces. I found another whole strange language one day while out looking for a cool pub. I rounded a bend in the road on my bicycle and came upon a meadow where lots of people were running around and a lot of people were watching. Some were sitting in lawn chairs and some were standing. It looked like some kind of a game so I stopped to watch. I asked a gentleman there what was going on. He replied 'a cricket match'. I asked if it had just started. He said, 'oh no, it started yesterday'. I said 'when will it be over?' He said, 'Maybe today, maybe tomorrow.' I asked him if he would explain this silly game to me and he informed me that it was not a silly game.

# Norwich

Many airmen, when they had an opportunity would visit the large towns in the region, above all Norwich.
**Rudolph Howell:**

I went back to town yesterday afternoon. It is a story in itself. I went down and lined up for the bus. I waited about twenty minutes for the bus. I was #51 in line and after the bus

*This spread:* Norwich children enjoy a Rodeo put on by American servicemen at the Norwich City Football ground at Carrow Road, 7 August 1943.

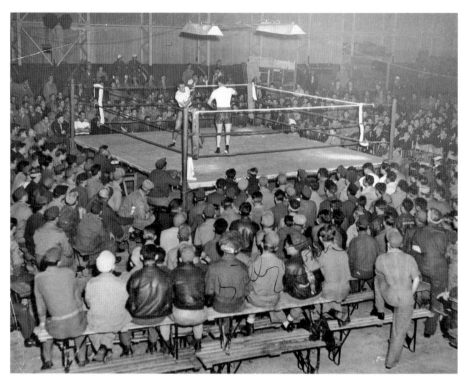

*Above and below:* Billy Conn, the 'Pittsburgh Kid', in action.

finally arrived they let 50 get on. So I caught a ride on a wrecker that was going to a small town about three miles away. I told him to let me off on the main highway so I could catch the civilian bus, but he forgot and took me all the way in town. So I walked about a mile to the bus stop and waited about twenty minutes for the civilian bus. It finally came by but was going the wrong way. I waited about fifteen minutes more and it finally came back but it was so crowded the driver didn't stop, so I walked back about half a mile and just happened to stumble across five other guys who had hired a cab so I hopped in and finally got over to the main town after about two hours of trying. I went to town for the specific purpose of buying about a dozen articles, chief of which was a radio. So after the horrible journey I finally straggled down the main drag and looked at the little signs in the stores saying, 'We close on Thursdays'. Every store in town was closed.

## Ken Jones:

I twisted my own arm and got an overnight pass for Norwich. Our open air shower stalls with the cold water in winter was hard to take and I looked forward to a hot bath. Catching a bus into Norwich, I checked into the Bethel Street Red Cross Club and was assigned a cot for the night. Then a lingering hot bath and shave with pounding on the door and shouts of 'Hurry Up'. Dressing hurriedly, I applied a little Lilac Vegital shaving lotion and hit the street for a bit of chow; then plotted a course to Harry's Pub. Some bomber crews were 'having a go' at a pint of 'alf and 'alf, with the pub crowd in a very sociable mood. I ordered a pint.

The 'Liberty Run' (Jack Preston).

**Clayton Wiseman:**

> 9 May Off on pass at 12.15 and in Norwich at 13.15. Saw a swell show, *Thousands Cheer*. Nashwinter, Ankoviak and Davis go Pub crawling and got stinking on gin and beer. Ank, and Nash put Davis and me to bed.
>
> 10 May: Got up at 9.30 feeling rough and wanting food, starved and thirsty. Ate in the YMCA. Sausage, toast, jelly and awful coffee. Dinner of Beef, potatoes, peas and coffee. We left Norwich at 15.00 and got back to camp about 16.30.

**Curtis Anderson:** 'Am going to Samson's tonight, a very nice place, so I hear.' On the next day, he wrote: 'Had a pretty good time last night. The place looked almost American and most everybody there were Americans. Still raining since last night.' After another visit to the Samson, he commented: 'I thought I was going to have to get a guide to find my way back to camp last night, it was so foggy.'

**James Chew**, at Horsham:

> When we arrived at the Samson and Hercules ballroom, the place was crowded with American GIs and their English girl friends. An orchestra on the Stage was playing popular, romantic tunes, and it had the 'Big Band' sound. Once in a while they played a fast number, and American GIs and English girls jitterbugged all over the Ballroom. Peggy and I took a table near the dance floor and watched the girls and GIs dance the fast tune they were playing. After the fast number was over, the Band began playing a slow, sweet tune. They sounded just like Glenn Miller, my favourite Band! And they were playing my favourite song! I asked Peggy to dance. She slid into my arms and we began gliding across the dance floor. She held herself close to me and put her cheek next to mine.

**John Rex**, military policeman:

> Business Operations were conducted from the Old Plough Inn on the corner of Market and Farmer Avenues across from the castle. The detention centre was on the second floor of this building, and if for any reason we had to keep a soldier in custody it was here, his organization was notified and its base military police would arrive and assume custody. Within 24 hours the soldier would be processed and returned to his base. That building is the La Rouen Restaurant today... My lighter moments were spent at the movies, the Haymarket Theatre, Samson and Hercules, and most often at the Lido. Rarely did I do any pub crawling. It was at the Lido I met a girl I could dance with quite effortlessly. We could really cut it! I have never danced so well since. There was boating on the River Yare, fish and chips, the military parades at Carrow Field, fun at the Haymarket shows. I loved Norwich.

Not all men wanted dancing and girls. Older, married men might find friendships, some of which lasted long after the war. **Harry Royal**, and his wife **Ivy** ran the Barn

Dance band at Seething.

Dancing to the Shipdham Hep Cats!

Tavern on the Dereham Road. The pub was severely damaged in the Baedeker raids of April 1942 and they continued trading in a temporary wooden building. They had two sons, Tony and Micky, and the family struck up a lasting friendship with several American servicemen, such as Edward 'Chick' Pell and his wife Cele. Correspondence between the families continued until Pell's death in an accident in 1962. **Bill Sadlier** also became a family friend. Bill's wife Ruth wrote to Ivy:

> I'm so glad Bill has a nice place to stay and I think it is so nice of you to do so much for him. I know we both appreciate it very much and it means a lot to Bill to have a little home life while he is away from our own home. You see he always enjoyed staying at home. He never was one to do much going out especially since we have been married. He told me all about your dear little boys and he enjoys being with the children. I know he is very lonely.

After the war, Bill wrote to Harry and Ivy: 'I want to thank you all for the lovely time I had in town and for all the hospitality you both showed me during my stay in England. I had a wonderful time and only hope that we can meet again in the future.'

Such family visits could bring up the problem anticipated before the Americans came over, as expressed by **John Rhoads**:

> Very likely the host used up the entire weekly rations for the family to see that the guest was properly entertained. Later, a system was worked out by the American military so a serviceman invited into a British home could draw meat and other foodstuff from the mess hall to ease the strain upon the host's food situation.

## Other 'Liberty Run' Towns

**Dick Bastien** (492 BG) at North Pickenham:

> King's Lynn was our liberty run town and to get there one would have to dress in his class A's, jump into the back of an army 6×6 and make the forty minute windy ride from North Pickenham. There were a few shops there but we could get all our things on base so the main attraction was the pubs and the people. It was fun to chat with someone different, not in uniform, and get his viewpoint, especially over a pint in the pub. The British reserve was hard to penetrate but when one succeeded one found them very interesting. After the pubs were closed we would stroll towards the square where the trucks were parked, buying a portion of Fish and Chips along the way, very tasty after a pint or two and so different from the mess hall food. It was summer and with double British Summer Time the afterglow of the sunset lasted almost until 11 p.m.

Hotels offered a little luxury after the conditions on the bases. **Roland Sabourin** recalled:

I think one of the greatest things I used to look forward to was a couple of days off and go to King's Lynn or someplace where you could stay in a hotel and get cleaned up, have a couple nice meals and some good beer. Just kind of enjoy yourself before you got back onto the base and be living under those conditions.

**Roy Jonasson:**

This being my day off I went into town this afternoon and went to the Methodist church in the evening and just came back on the 8:30 bus. I certainly enjoyed the services and so many things came to me as I sat there. This was their Harvest Sunday when they give thanksgiving for the Harvest and the food that they have received. The church was decorated so prettily with golden rod, Indian paint brushes, dahlias, and in front of the altar vegetables and fruits had been placed all about on the tables and floor. The pastor really preached a very good sermon and the choir was very good.

Rationing had to be borne in mind, of course. **Rudolph Howell** in the nearest town:

At three o'clock Deleot and I stepped into a small restaurant for a spot of tea. We really got more than a spot, we got a whole teapot full. It was so hot it burned the hair off my tongue. Deleot also ordered tongue salad. I didn't care for that so I just asked the girl to bring me some kind of pastry. So she brought back two small cakes and I had tea and crumpets. I was really getting Anglicized. The cakes were very good, being filled with whipped cream. I was good enough to let Deleot taste one and he liked it very well, too. We both decided we wanted more. That's where I made my first blunder. I stopped the girl and very casually asked her for two more orders of the cakes. She looked shocked at first, then said, 'I'm sorry, sir, but we only allow one cake to a customer. One of those was yours and one was the other officer's'. I had eaten them both, of course, so I felt pretty silly.

## The Public House

The official *Handbook* explained the ritual of the public house:

You are welcome in the British pubs as long as you remember one thing. The pub is the 'poor man's club', the neighbourhood or village gathering place, where the men have come to see their friends, not strangers. If you want to join a darts game, let them ask you first (as they probably will). And if you are beaten it is the custom to stand aside and let someone else play.

**Myron Keilman** (392 BG), based at Wendling recalled his practical experience of the English 'local':

The beer as I remember came by the names of stout, mild and bitter, half and half, and nut brown ale. It was served from casks at room temperature. Some of us never developed a taste for it. To say the least, none of it resembled our US of A brands of cold lager, pilsner or bach. The pubs, depending on rationing availability, also featured light war-time snacks of sandwiches or fish and chips. The always prominent and well-worn dart board was available for fun and games. The loser bought the beer. The darts were available from the inn-keeper for three pence or so. Of course, the beer was rationed: thus the pubs closed down at 10 p.m. to conserve beer, electricity and coke for heating. At closing time – regardless of the activities – the pub-keeper would call, 'Time, Gentlemen Please'. With that, everyone 'bottomed out', sang 'Knees Up, Mother Brown' and filed out.

**John Rhoads** recalled the public house ritual:

We sat back, supped our ale and relaxed. Occasionally we were invited to join our British cousins in a game of darts or bowling on the green behind the pub. To 'crash' a game uninvited was socially taboo and rude. Invitations came when the patrons got to know us and to observe how we conducted ourselves.

The men of 389 BG at Hethel favoured the Green Dragon in Wymondham, a traditional old-world English hostelry; the nickname of the Bomb Group became the 'Green Dragons'!

## The Red Cross

The American Red Cross Services to the Armed Forces (SAF) operated a club service wherever American troops were located overseas. It provided refreshments, accommodation, comfort and recreational activities to servicemen. The Red Cross staffed and supplied permanent service clubs, travelling clubmobiles, and other recreational facilities around the world. At its peak, the Red Cross operated nearly 2,000 such facilities abroad, staffed by 5,000 Red Cross workers, mostly women, and approximately 140,000 volunteers, many of whom were local people. Red Cross clubs in Norwich included the Bishop's Palace and St Andrew's Hall.

## Girls

Naturally, many of the young men wanted to meet girls, and many long-term relationships were formed between American airmen and British women.

**John van Acker:**

You asked about the English girls. They are about the only English we come in contact with except in stores etc. We have a liberty run, which is a bunch of trucks, that goes

The English pub (Jack Preston).

The Green Dragon, Wymondham, sketch by Ludwig Lund: The nickname of the 389 BG, the 'Green Dragons', was supposedly taken from this pub.

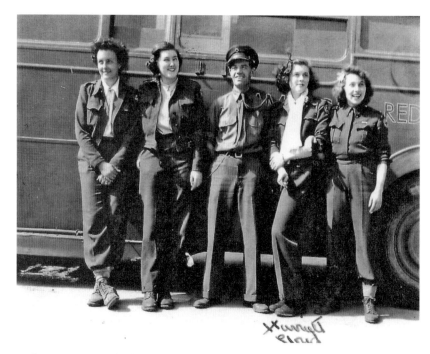

Red Cross personnel of a 'donut wagon': from left to right: unknown girl; Anne
Tunnecliffe, the only English girl on the wagon; unknown man; girl whose
signature appears to read Harriet Floyd; Sally Ann Peters.

St Andrew's Hall, used by the American Red Cross.

to a town called King's Lynn. It is not very large but quite old with narrow winding streets and we go there once or twice a week now when it is warm to dance or go to a movie. English girls as a whole are dumber than Americans mainly because education over here is fairly poor. They only go to school about seven years. Also everything here is backward. Most English girls do strike me as being more conservative and practical than American girls. They are definitely plainer and are satisfied with much less than American girls. Also they are quite willing to put up with a lot of waiting etc. as flying sort of stops the boys from going to town. Well, those are my observations – you can take them for what they are worth.

**Alfred Neumunz** to Babs: 'Whenever we go to town I don't guess we meet the best people, in fact that's for sure.' In another letter: 'The girls here are strictly eager and mercenary. So far my only contacts have been a few quips in a local pub. It's no fun when I have you to compare them with – there just isn't any comparison.'

**Paul Steichen**: 'One of our gunners – Barker – has met some English girl and is going strong for her and wants to marry her. Enlisted men have to wait something like 60 days before they can get married after they make application so maybe he will change his mind by then.' (Barker did indeed get married.)

**Willis Marshall** tells the story of a romance between an American GI and a British girl:

We found that we could get a 48 hour pass. This would be our first pass since early October at San Francisco, two months prior. Ken Nicholson and I decided to head for town on the seven o'clock liberty run. These trucks left the base every night at seven and departed Norwich promptly at eleven. If you missed that 11 p.m. departure it was either start hoofing it or a cab. It was just about 12 miles back to Hethel. When Ken and I arrived in Norwich it was a cold, misty night so we decided to head for the Red Cross Club. We obtained directions and found our way to that club. Since it was our first night in town we booked a crib for the night, at a cost of 25 cents. Actually we paid in English currency which was one shilling, five pence. We sacked in, I believe just after eight and shortly thereafter we heard a lot of noise and commotion. We decided to get up and see what was going on. Turned out there was a Red Cross dance that evening so we decided to attend. We found that we had to have tickets that were available at the Cathedral. This was about a block or so away. We knew that we couldn't get lost so we went and got our tickets. When we returned to the basement of the Red Cross an orchestra was in full swing. We descended the steps and almost immediately a hostess was at our side. She sensed or knew that we were newcomers and introduced herself. She then called Lillian Blake and introduced us. She took us over to a group of girls, introduced us to her two girlfriends, a Charlotte (Dotte) Venis, and her sister Eileen. I immediately had a feeling about Dotte and this made a tremendous impact on my future. In time she became my loving wife. Since neither Ken nor I could dance we sat and conversed with these girls, at least when they weren't out on the floor. In reality this was most of the time. Ken and I decided to see if we could walk these girls home so at the end of dancing we were waiting at the coat room. We asked them if we could and with a short conference between them they gave us the O.K. So, off we started out, not knowing that they were out to teach us a lesson. After about two miles and many turns Ken and I decided that we would never find our way back in that misty pitch blackness. The lesson that they wanted to teach us was that they went the long way to their home which was over five miles, while in reality they lived just about three miles. These limeys really could walk, and didn't seem to mind it one bit. We asked Dotte and Eileen for a date for the next evening, and they consented to meet us at the Red Cross. We were there and lo and behold they arrived at the agreed time. Dotte told me later that they used to make dates and never show up, just to get rid of the pestering Yanks. Ken and I double dated for several weeks. Then he decided that he was going to stay on the base. He spent his free time flat on his back, hands under his head, and staring at the ceiling. I guess that it was a form of what we called being flak happy. It was just his way of coping … I continued to date Dotte and started spending all the time I could away from the base, with a lot of that time at her home. Her family accepted me very well and made me a home away from home. Along with her sister, she had two older brothers and two younger ones. The two older brothers were with the British Armed Forces.

Dotte and I had become engaged and I had obtained permission from my parents to get married. I had to have permission because I was still under 21 years of age. We also had to have a meeting with the chaplain. I set up an appointment with Chaplain Mellish, went to Norwich and met Dotte. We caught a bus to Wymondham and walked to the base. We met with the chaplain and things were well on the way to start setting up a wedding date. The wheels turned slow and they tried to discourage weddings between the yanks and British. This all happened during the month of April 1945. It turned out that the wedding wouldn't be able to take place until February 1947. I was returned to the US before permission came down through the channels. Dot had to now start through immigration to get to the US. With a lot of headaches, problems and perseverance, she finally arrived in New York on February 3rd 1947. We were married the next day.

It is estimated that more than 70,000 British women went to the United States with their American husbands after the war. In early 1946, as part of 'Operation War Bride', the United States Army transported thousands of war brides and children from Britain to America, the first group arriving in February 1946. Some brides had already moved to the States. Lillian Williams of the post office in Bury St Edmunds married Sergeant Jones of East Moline and moved there in 1944. As the local press reported,

Mrs Jones finds it difficult to realise that one can enter a store in the United States and purchase almost anything, so accustomed has she been to the strict rationing and the scarcity of many articles in Britain, where even handkerchiefs are rationed. Sergt Jones (still in England) has become a devotee of the typical English dinner fare roast beef and Yorkshire pudding. Rationing has had only the best effects upon the baby, whose name is Diane Cheryl Margaret.

There were also weddings within the USAAF community, one of which was witnessed by **Mary Williams-Elder:**

24 September 1944: Jean Young married Joe Majors yesterday, and it was lovely. But, to begin at the beginning. We arrived at the church en masse – via truck – and our barracks was on the front row. The organist played in his best style, and then the processional began – out came Joe and his best man and two ushers – the organist kept on playing – but no bride. Finally, after the processional had been played about three times the Minister came out and announced the bride was a little late. I wish you could have seen Joe's face – it was so funny. Well, we sat for about fifteen more minutes and waited. Finally the bride arrived and everything proceeded according to schedule. First came Peaches – she was adorable in pink, with the cutest hat you ever saw. Her flowers were shaking so I was afraid she was going to drop them, but she made it OK. Then came Reimer, she was in lavender – and looked just as sweet as could be. Then Emmy came – she was in blue – all three of them had the most set smiles on their faces – just like they were afraid to breathe – which I guess they were. Finally, the bride arrived. She looked prettier than I've ever seen her. Joe looked at her

US Bride: Jean Young on her marriage to Joe Mayers.

like – well, aren't you ashamed of yourself. Hal (his best man) told me later that the first thing Joe said to Jean when she finally got to the altar was 'you know I've been thru this once before'. The sun was shining during the whole ceremony and the light from one of the windows was directly on the bridal couple – it was really a beautiful sight to see. The minister was old, and grey headed – just as sweet as could be, and he made the ceremony really mean something. His prayer at the end of the service was excellent.

Many of these marriages took place in the girl's local parish church, which might well be close to the airbase: to take just one example among many, Reg Hunt and Joan Moore married at Seething parish church on 29 March 1945. Some marriages took place in other churches: Norwich Cathedral was favoured by many American servicemen, including Earl Zimmerman (389 BG), who married June Courtenay there in March 1945. Others might choose the Roman Catholic church (now Cathedral) of St John the Baptist in Norwich, where Captain Edward Israel (448 BG) married Miriam Thorpe. Other couples might prefer the local registry office. In at least one case, the marriage was conducted over the transatlantic telephone! Marvin Kite (44 BG) was already back in the United States when he married Doris, then in London, over the phone in November 1946 – their formal marriage took place in March 1947 when Doris had finally crossed the pond herself. Although most of the GI brides naturally emigrated for a new life with their husband in his home town, in a few cases the couple preferred to stay in Norfolk.

# Chapter Eight

# Sightseers

For almost all of the Americans, this was their first trip 'across the pond', and, while many were happy to enjoy the entertainment officered on the bases and on their liberty run trips to dances in the larger towns, others were more determined sightseers. The coast and countryside of Norfolk had a lot to offer.
**Rudolph Howell:**

> The roads (at least the ones I've seen) are very narrow and winding and they really wind you over some pretty countryside ... And all through the countryside, especially where I am now, you can see thatched roofs, something I have never seen before. And since I have been here I haven't seen even one house built of wood.

**Mary Williams-Elder:**

> We were taken to an English estate to tea. I've seen movies of such places but never expected to be really at one. There was a church on the grounds – a moat – but it was filled in with flowers now. The house was so old it had two or three types of architecture in it. The lawns – well – my first thought was green velvet.

We have seen how men were attracted to Norwich by the dances. Some were more into cultural sightseeing.
**Roy Jonasson:**

> One evening during the holiday week I managed to go in and see a stage show, an English pantomime, Cinderella. It was wonderful! The English are tops in this kind of play, especially pantomimes. It was at the Royal Theatre here in town and they have put on such a play for the *last 300 years at the same place*. Of course, the building has been remodelled and part of it re-built. During the program they (the audience) sing old English songs so all of us had a really good time. They had little girls (ages 8 to 12 yrs) take the part of fairies and they actually winged out into the air away from the stage supported by thin wires. The scenery was wonderful; the golden carriage that Cinderella rode in was very pretty and the actors and actresses, though of local talent, acted like professionals. I have never seen anything like it. It lasted for three and one-half hours

Norwich Cathedral Close seen from a B-24.

The airman as sightseer: Pull's Ferry in the snow.

Launching a sailing boat made from a wing tank.

and cost 2 schillings and 6 pense [*sic*] (50 cents). I had a good seat. While I was there I wished that you could have been with me and could have seen it. I want to take you to those kind of plays and shows when I get back for I know that you will love them. They had such lovely, restful music throughout. Tubby and Cinderella and the two ugly sisters played their parts very well.

**Roy Jonasson,** on another occasion:

Yesterday was my day off and I went in to town and had a good hot shower. I believe I must have stayed under it for a half an hour. In the afternoon I visited 'Stranger's Hall', an old English Building dating back about 300 years. It consisted of many rooms, halls, bed and living rooms, dining rooms, all just as one would find them years ago with all the old-style furniture. The 'Hall' or 'Building' is where the Lord Mayor lived and where strangers visiting the village stayed overnight. Down in the basement was located the servants' quarters, the old carriages and horses' stables. There were so many things to see that one could go back many times and still enjoy it.

I also visited one of the two oldest Shakesperian [*sic*] Theaters in England and it was very interesting. It had the old balcony around three sides, old seats and tall wooden posts. There were no curtains and they told us the actors made the announcements. We saw the prompter's seat. I know you would have noticed many more things about the theater than I because you are much better read. How I wish you could have been along.

I have become acquainted with a Mr Green who was born in Norwich and knows of all these interesting places and their histories and, of course, that makes it more interesting. His wife is an invalid and confined part of the time to bed, but she seems to be getting better. She was a Blitz casualty.

I stopped at their home last night and it was small but lovely. In their small dining room they had two large French doors that opened to their back yard which was all in green grass and flowers and fruit trees (around the border and edge of the lot). It was a lovely sight to see and such a view when looking out. I thought of our new home and how nice one can make it with little effort and management.

For supper we had strawberries which are just coming in now [letter written 6 July]. They sell at 1s 8d a basket (36 cents), the same size as our basket at home. On the berries they use an English custard sauce which is very good. Then we had slices of bread with butter spread thin, and tea. I did enjoy the day so much.

### Rudolph Howell:

I did go into town last Sunday afternoon. I got there at 1 p.m. and we left at 4.40 p.m. I may have stayed longer if there had been anything to do, but it seems that *everything* is closed on Sunday except the pubs, and there is a pub on both sides of the street in every block. Back home we have two or three filling stations on every other street corner. In Town (and it is a fairly large town, about the size of Macon, I believe) I saw three filling stations in all my wanderings, and two of them were closed permanently. However, there were millions of pubs. They say the Sunday is family day over here, and if you don't have a family you may as well not venture into town. It seemed to be the truth.

Parsons and I went in together. We walked all over town and believe me we were tired when it was over. We spent most of our time just looking in windows and seeing the prices of things ... We saw some men's suits for about $25 (they still wear cuffs on their pants). Work shoes were about $7 a pair. We found a table radio about the size of our record player back home for about $45.

They went to the Castle Museum:

It had a great many interesting things. I saw the rompers worn by Edward VII when he was just a little young 'un. I also saw a very plain and drab blue and white dress worn by Marie Antoinette. She really must have been a slick chick in that outfit. There were all kinds of stuffed animals and about a million kinds of stuffed birds. They had all kinds of stone and bronze implements reminiscent of the prehistoric and early days of England ... It was all very interesting to me and next chance I get I'm going back and spend a little time there.

On another occasion, he visited a city church, probably St Peter Mancroft:

> You can see by the leaflet that the church is 490 years old, being built thirty seven years before Columbus discovered America … It was all very interesting. The wall is covered with stones placed in memory of various people. The floor is made up of great stone slabs each with an inscription on it telling who it commemorates. There was a huge figure in the back but I was unable to make out what it represented or what was its purpose. The church doesn't seem to be too well kept and it certainly isn't modern, but I suppose it is very difficult to keep a place like that looking spic and span, especially in wartime.

**Delmar Johnson** at Wendling: 'Our liberty runs were to King's Lynn … somebody there once pointed out the house where Captain Vancouver had lived.' Johnson was especially interested as his wife, Lucille, was raised in Vancouver, Washington.

**Roy Jonasson:**

> I have been spending the first part of my furlough here at Yarmouth (Greater), a coastal town along the North Sea. I really like it here as there is a very good ocean breeze which seems to make one feel so good.
>
> Yarmouth reminds me of Balboa Beach a lot except there are no concessions and it is not commercialized. Many of the buildings and homes have been destroyed but the people go on as usual about their business and chores … Here at Yarmouth I spend most of my time eating, sleeping and going down to the pier to watch the boats come and go and the fishermen. I am having such a grand time.

**Alfred Neumunz**, 5 November 1944:

> Have been away for several days on a pass. Lately they've been exceptionally kind to us and passes have been coming regularly. Ever since switching crews my writing has been next to nil – I've been moody as all hell not even good company for myself but with a few days off – a little booze, and everything's back to normal once again.
>
> We visited a small town on the ocean, Gt Yarmouth. It is quite free of Yanks and we had a fine time. We were very fortunate in meeting several girls who make wonderful company, the first English I've met who aren't the ordinary riff-raff that a soldier usually meets. They've had wonderful educations and make the average American girl look sick. Ours is but a purely platonic relationship but a friendship that I'll value while I'm over here. I learned more about England and Europe in the few days spent with them than in the previous two months over here. This part of the world is truly a fascinating place and I sure hope to visit England and Europe come peace. It brings home the truth that Americans are really a dull bunch – whose lives begins and ends with the dollar.
>
> Honey, the world is still a pretty wonderful place and if nothing else the army has taught me there's so much to live for, see, and learn – all of which I'd like to accomplish with you for more and more I realize how wonderful you really are.

**'Andy' Anderson:**

19 Aug 1944: Spent the day at Wraxham [*sic*, Wroxham is the correct spelling] on the Broads. Spam, potted meat, pastry, orange juice, oranges and candy for my lunch. Water too cold to enjoy. Some bike ride back, rained on twice, headwind so hard I couldn't make much headway. I was out when I got back to the camp, about a 12 mile ride.

1 Sep 1944: Went to the seaside. Cramer got a 3rd class ticket but rode 1st class all the way. 3rd class were loaded, not much difference. Beach was very rocky, barbed wire still all along the beach. Water and wind too cold for swimming. Pretty nice day.

Others had relatives or connections in England to visit. **Lyndon Allen** went to see Myrtle Moore, the wife of a friend of his brother who lived with her sister at Leigh-on-Sea:

On one visit Mrs Moore insisted that I let her know in advance before I was to come into London the next time, and she would have a knuckle of beef for dinner. I did so anticipating a soup bone for dinner. But I wasn't worried, it was the desire of wanting to serve me dinner that impressed me. When I found out what a knuckle of beef was, a small very nice roast, I was truly humbled, I wondered how many weeks of meat ration points these ladies had used to afford me a dinner at their home.

Naturally, London was the great attraction for those with a two or three day 'furlough'.

**Robert Boyle:**

26 July 1944: I just got back from London after spending 2 days there. As usual I didn't do much. I slept most of the time. I stayed at the Savoy hotel again, and no kidding, the beds are so soft that you almost need a periscope to see over the edge of it. I went to a show the second night, it was pretty good but nothing to rave about.

**J. Ray Bickel:**

In London, after dinner we went to the Savoy Theater and saw *The Last of Mrs Chaney*, a horrible English play. The British people laughed while I was bored stiff … After that I sat in the hotel lounge after dodging the Piccadilly commandos (prostitutes in Piccadilly Circus who tried to lure us into their apartments for sex).

**Ken Jones:**

On the morning of April 7th [1945] we showered, shaved and polished shoes and brass. We dressed in Class 'A' uniforms for the first time in ages … [We] looked sharp and smelled good 'if I do say so old chap'.

The musette shoulder bag was packed with tooth brush, razor, a change of soxs [*sic*], underwear, two clean shirts and three Red Dot (rum-soaked) cigars from the PX.

*Above and next page:* Two American views of London: Piccadilly Circus; London bomb damage.

Copilot, navigator, bombardier and I were headed out for an English 'holiday' to the legendary city of London.

We hailed a taxi at the station and headed for the center of London. At the driver's suggestion, he dropped us off at a quaint little bed and board town house. This boarding house became our base of operations. The landlord served tea and biscuits for breakfast and that was the only food we could get there. The rooms were clean and there were sheets on the bed. (What a luxury!) We didn't have sheets at the 389th.

The heat source was small radiator type heater that operated for one half hour if you put a shilling in the coin slot. This was somewhat better compared to our air base. Still, the room was cold … Our town house was within walking distance of Piccadilly Circus and Trafalgar Square (maybe two miles). We checked into the first pub for a pint of 'relaxant' for anti-freeze purposes and to interrogate the Yank customers about what sights we should see in our limited time. Having determined what we wanted to know, we went into a war-time restaurant for a meal of soggy fish and 'tay' (tea) … The big thing for snacks here is 'fish and chips' and I can't cut that. The chips are French fried potatoes. They taste like raw wet noodles soaked in rainwater.'

We popped into a pub for a wee drop of stimulant, to rest and to kill some time before the evening performance at the Windmill theatre. All the visiting Yanks gave the Windmill rave notices – it was one thing you should see before you die.

This was a variety show with many beautiful women: 'they poised as statuettes, remaining motionless. Under English law women can pose in the buff but cannot move about on the stage. As the English say, It was naughty but nice and – slightly more than smashing!'

**Joseph Nathan:**

We got rooms at the Jules Club as soon as we got to town. We were starved and ate as soon as we could, tried to get into a show, but were too late, and finally wound up at a dance at the Duchess Club. But we were even too late for that and the only girls we met were the Piccadilly Commandos who were out in droves propositioning every Yank that passed. We got past them though, and back to the Jules for the first hot bath we'd had in weeks. I filled the tub to the brim as hot as I could take it and then soaked for an hour until the sweat ran off my brow and my fingers shriveled up from being in the water too long. It was wonderful and followed by a soft warm bed with clean sheets, it was the perfect way to spend an evening.

**John Rex:**

I walked around in awe of the old city of London taking in the sights and riding the great underground, just for the fun of riding it. Looked in on St Paul's and was overwhelmed by it. Took pictures of all those places. I really preferred Hammersmith. It was less crowded, the atmosphere and the girls were more to my liking. One particular girl was there just about every time I was, I usually searched her out. We danced quite well together. Besides, there was a custom in England that was not practiced back in the States, girls cut in on girls. Good grief, how much of an ego builder does a guy need.

**Robert Doyle:**

Since writing you last I had a 48-hr pass which I spent in London. It is quite a city, resembles New York at times, except it doesn't have the high buildings. We had a swell time there, and didn't spend much either. However, he failed to find a gift for a birthday present: Everything here is rationed, and what isn't rationed either isn't available or isn't worth having … The taxis are quaint. Old looking hacks that give you a laugh at first.. Also they have double decker trolleys, like our double decker buses. They have buses and a subway system too. All in all, it's the same as any other place … The big difference is at night. Naturally every night, all night is blackout time, so we saw no great white way like Times Square etc, and it really gets dark. I guess they are used to that by now though.

**Doyle,** on a second visit: 'We had rooms in the Savoy Hotel, and was it ritzy. It is one of the best hotels in the world, and really nice. While in London we went swimming, looked around a bit, and had a couple of good dinners, as far as that is possible in London.'

His family queried the swimming so he expanded on it: 'It was outdoors in Hyde Park on the Serpentine River. There are bathing facilities there, and it was very nice.' Such visits might highlight the different cultures once more.

**Paul Steichen:**

London or any other English town differs a bit from American cities in that stores are just a little different. The store I visited was the biggest in a certain town, not London, and I made a purchase of the only bracelet they had at the counter which dispenses bracelets. Whether it's the war to blame or not, I guess the stocks are depleted a bit.

**Dick Bastien:**

In London were establishments called 'The Brasserie' which I thought dealt in women's undies until shown they were really posh cafeterias. Once I remember we went to Claridge's, a really posh hotel, and ordered a meal off a menu we couldn't read. Everything was first rate, gleaming silverware on snow white tables, napkins, crystal drinking equipment, the whole shebang. When the entrée was served it came by cart covered over with a silver dome, very impressive. It turned out to be a slice of spam! We actually laughed which of course showed the other diners that these brash Americans didn't have the typical British reserve and good manners. To further demonstrate our ignorance we laced the spam with loads of Colman's yellow mustard, it turned out to be quite hot, nearly rendering our dinner inedible. It was only after much scraping and copious pitchers of water that we choked it down. I imagine the waiters and kitchen help were laughing as hard as we were.

**Rudolph Howell:**

The only intelligent looking thing in sight was a couple of British MPs (military policemen) so I crossed over an asked one of them where I might catch a cab. Well I've been over here long enough that I can understand this lingo OK with little or no trouble, but it seems that I accosted the wrong bird this time. He had the most terrific accent and incomprehensible dialect I have yet encountered. Out of the jumble of words that he let out, most of which he repeated two or three times to be sure I understood him, I finally gathered that he was saying something about it would be nearly impossible to catch a cab round there, but I could catch a bus across the street. So I thanked him and crossed over. I know I waited at least half an hour before my bus came by. I noticed by the other buses that they didn't stop on every corner but only when a red light caught them so I walked down to the middle of the block so I would be able to catch it at either corner. Eventually it did come and I had to run for it but I got it. I asked the girl what the price was and she said it depended on where I was going. It was the first time I had ever ridden a city bus that you couldn't get on and ride anywhere you wanted to for the same price. It was the same way with the subway. In New York you could ride all over the city for a nickel, but in London the price depended on where you were going.

**Herk Taylor:**

For our first R & R leave we had to go to the 'Big Smoke', London. Naturally we went to Piccadilly Circus but couldn't find a room so we called around and found one out in Russell Square. We 'flew the tube' out there late at night and when we had checked in had our first encounter with quaint English sayings. The young lady behind the desk asked us, 'What time do you want to be knocked up in the morning?' I saw my Navigator blush and the others just looked at one another.

**John van Acker**, 11 March 1945:

I do get a kick out of the Englishman's habit of eating, but it was probably more amusing when I tried it myself! They hold the fork in the left hand and with the right a knife is used to cut and push food upon top of the bottom of the fork. Confusing isn't it? I thought so too while testing the method out. Grandmother would be proud! All their cups are real tiny, with a spoon to match.

London had suffered greatly during the blitz. That was over by the time the Americans were here, but there was a new danger from the summer of 1944 onwards, the V-1's and V-2's, Hitler's last attempt to subjugate Londoners. Many servicemen experienced them.

**'Andy' Anderson** went to London and got a room at the Great Eastern Hotel: 'Saw all the sights, St Paul's, House of Parliament, 10 Downing St. Buzz bomb hit about three blocks, sure shook the ground ... Left London on July 1st [1944] about 1300. Trains packed with people getting away from the bombs. Held a little baby part of the way, some lady had 4 children taking them to the country.'

On a later trip, he noted that he 'really went through Westminster Abbey. Saw one grave that dated back to 1064, most of the writing was worn off with so many feet walking over it. Saw *Wing and a Prayer* at the Odeon. A very good show. Ate at Trocadero. Went to the Palais de Dance at Hammer Smith.' The next day, he 'went to St Paul's, took me all morning. Went to see 'Cobra Lady', had dinner at 'L'Auberge De France' some place, had a very good meal. And a good night's sleep. Piccadilly was really crowded, nothing but uniforms.'

**Robert Boyle**, 6 August 1944:

So you have heard of the robot bombs in London. Well, they aren't good, however I fail to see their effectiveness as a military weapon. It's just like bowling, if you close your eyes, and heave the ball in the direction of the pins, you might hit something vital, but the chances are you'll hit one pin, or none. I can't see how they could ever do the damage that one of our missions does to them. We get a whole mess of planes, each with a number of bombs and aim at something. Well, if you are in the vicinity it's time to duck. I don't even worry about these robots. I've seen quite a few, and one was so close that when the engine stopped, I could actually hear the whistle it made, like a falling bomb. It hit the other side of the hotel I was in, and smashed a window in my room, but aside from scaring me momentarily, did nothing else. Besides, we bomb those robot installations too.

**Roy Jonasson:** 'As we were getting out of the cab to go in to Westminster Abbey, a rocket fell in the distance and the cab driver remarked, 'That's one less rocket!' and we went on our way. Good English humor.'

  **Herk Taylor:** 'Sometime in the middle of the night I found myself rudely knocked on the floor by a buzz bomb that made a direct hit on a bus in front of the hotel. There was also a direct hit on the Regent Palace that night. After flak and fighters in combat, we decided this was too much and left.'

  **Bob:**

You mentioned the robot planes, they don't bother me. I sleep right through them. Actually, it's almost pitiful to see the people sleeping on the floor in the subways etc. I don't envy them, but after you see what those bombs do, you can understand why the people want to get out of the way of them. Most of the population are very scared of them. They say it's worse than the 'blitz'. Really it isn't. They just can't comprehend it. As one fellow told me: 'Just think –nobody in it – weird isn't it' Oh well, it can't last too much longer, I don't believe.

# Chapter Nine

# Children

The Americans are remembered for their love of children, and their generosity towards them. The *Handbook* given to American soldiers in Britain says:

> Children the world over are easy to get along with. British children are much like our own. The British have reserved much of the food that gets through solely for their children. To the British children you as an American are 'something special'. For they have been fed at their schools and impressed with the fact that the food they ate was sent to them by Uncle Sam. You don't have to tell the British about lend-lease food, they know about it and appreciate it.

Whether or not they had children of their own back home, the airmen had a fully-deserved reputation for their kindness and generosity to local children. Many bases welcomed children, who were allowed to wander around much more freely than would have been permitted in English airbases. A little barter might be tried, as recalled by **Paul Steichen**: 'A couple of little English kids just came in looking for gum and candy. I tried to get some eggs from them but they don't have any.'

**John van Acker:**

> As we are quite far out in the country and it is difficult and uncomfortable travelling, we stay pretty close to the field. Consequently we don't have much to do with the British. One thing though while riding around on a bicycle I have seen a lot of children. All of them in every little village and at many crossroads are looking for candy and gum. Guess they never had any and most never had any sweets before the Americans came. They know the Yanks get candy & gum (rationed) from the PX so all the kids use the same somewhat classical, coined phrase, 'Any Gum Chum?' Can't help but feeling sorry for them.

**Rudolph Howell:**

> The most outstanding thing in town (and towns all over England) is the drove of kids (all seem to be not over eight and not under three) who are constantly coming up and asking, 'Got any gum, chum?' or 'Got any candy, Andy?' Occasionally they ask for a

Names of schools in America that had donated money to buy a plane.

threepenny (thrup'nny as they put it) to go to the show or to buy 'ices' (ice cream to you, and it's no good). And sometimes they get mad if you don't have what they ask for or you won't give it to them. One fellow was in town the other day and some kid asked him for gum. He said he didn't have any. The kid stepped back, looked at him very scornfully, and said, 'I hope you get sent to the South Pacific.' They're a tough little bunch over here.

## Roy Jonasson:

Yesterday was my day off so in the afternoon I went to town and saw the show *Tampico* and the other picture *Blondie and Dagwood*. I really enjoyed them and got a good many laughs from them.

Instead of riding the bus back I walked all the way, about ten miles, because I never did it before and wanted to see all of the little villages and countryside on the way. When you ride you go so fast. This time of the year [July] all of the flowers are out and the little English yards are beautiful with all colors, and the green grass, and all colors of roses. The children were playing about and they always have a good word for the Yank. One little girl playing in the road looked at me and said, 'Yank, would you please tell me the time as I have to go in the house as mother will be coming home from work at 6 p.m.'. Dear, I nearly picked her up and brought her home to you!

The parties the airmen held at Christmas became legendary in a land still blighted by strict rationing. Forty years later, **Frank Law** (448 BG) recalled:

The Christmas of 1944 spent at Seething is one that I shall never forget. Our military had a more or less mutual agreement with the Germans that no missions were to be flown on that day. We had several American Red Cross workers working with the English Red Cross workers and we had been told of the plan to pick up the children at a particular spot on base after they had been transported from the outlying areas and that the child was to be our guest for the entire day … Both the enlisted men and the officers had the same instructions for the Christmas Day celebration. I know that some of the military personnel had more than just one child in tow. However, I chose one boy as he got off the 6×6 truck and a close friend of mine took his brother. These were the Saunders boys – Teddy and Jimmy if I recall their names correctly.

All of the children were extremely well behaved that day and, needless to say, it made the day such a memorable one for all of us in what was then called the Army Air Corps. Most of us had saved our candy and chewing gum which we had received in packages from home. Sweets of any kind were most difficult to get here in the States at that time but our folks back home always managed to include some in the packages we received and we, in turn, saved our goodies for the English children.

On that day we had a feast fit for a King – roast turkey with all of the trimmings, as we say. The tables in our Officers' Mess were festooned with all sorts of good things to eat and this was also just as true for the enlisted men's mess hall.

We also had entertainment that day which included a moving picture and later a visit from Santa Claus (Father Christmas). The children enjoyed this immensely. There were also some additional gifts which I don't recall too specifically at this time. The theatre was so crowded that most of us held our little guests on our laps – I certainly did.

**Roy Jonasson, 23 December 1944:**

Yesterday we had a great number of English children at our base from the surrounding villages for a Christmas party. And what lovely children they were, so polite, clean, poor but so cheerful, and in old clothing though it was clean and neat. I can say that we men had as much fun as the children in having a good time. I nearly adopted one to bring back to you! And I love them just as much. Our trucks picked them up from the villages and brought them back. Many were orphan children. We had a Santa Claus for them and candy. For the last month we have been saving our candy that we get at the PX.

Everywhere one goes he finds the American soldier putting on a Christmas party for the children, both here and in France. Yes, we continue stronger than ever with our work and operations but this is a little of the real Christmas spirit given to our Allies, especially to those who have nothing, or have lost much. What a great day it will be for all when we get peace once and for all and we can come back to the ones we love and miss so much.

On Christmas Eve in 1944, 453 BG at Old Buckenham played host to more than 1,250 British children, aged between four and fourteen. They came from nearby towns and

*This spread:* Christmas with 448 BG.

villages but included London evacuees staying there, some of whom were orphans. However, the airmen had even more ambitious plans. Since November they had planned to send a plane across to France to act as Santa Claus to the French children. Local children and the airmen both contributed toys, Christmas cards and candy. The British children were divided into three groups:

Those between four and seven were entertained at the Aero Club, given stockings filled with candy and toys, by Father Christmas, and served ice cream and coke.

Those between seven and eleven were taken outside and shown the planes, and the gifts for the French children were handed over. An eleven-year-old orphan of the blitz, Judith McDonald, christened the plane that was to act as Santa's sleigh, giving it the name *Liberty Run*. Unfortunately the plane slipped off the runway and the launch had to be postponed until the following day.

Meanwhile those aged between eleven and fourteen were taken to the base theatre and kept entertained by Cpl Sissenstein of Special Services, who was an amateur magician, and were then joined by the younger children who had been outside, to see cartoons. They all went to the Aero Club for gifts, ice cream, candy and cakes.

The next day – Christmas Day – the 'Liberty Run' flew to France and the gifts were distributed to French children at Rainbow Corner in Paris by Santa Claus himself.

British children at an airbase Christmas party, 24 December 1944.

Father Christmas with an American accent: a French child receiving a gift in Paris, Christmas 1944.

**John Rowe** at Seething, Christmas 1944: 'Seething airbase entertained a host of refugee children away from their homes in the war zones on this Christmas day. They had turkey, pumpkin pie and all the trimmings. Many had 2 or 3 helpings.'

Letters to Capt McLaughlin, the Special Services Officer at Attlebridge, show much the hospitality was appreciated:

From **the Superintendent of Dr Barnardo's Homes, Honingham,** 31 December 1943:

Please convey to all the Officers and enlisted men my deep thanks for the entertainment and treat they gave the children on Christmas Eve.

To those who gave their rations of candies and cookies and to all who worked in the preparing of the food, Thank You.

It was greatly enjoyed by the children and I know it will be remembered for years.

May God bless you all, and may the New Year hasten the coming of a lasting peace.

From **St Andrew's Hospital, Thorpe,** 10 January 1944:

I am requested by the Visiting Committee to extend to you their sincere appreciation of your kindness in bringing over a party of musicians and entertainers to the Emergency section of this Hospital at Christmas. The entertainment was very much appreciated by the patients and my Committee desire to express to you all, their grateful thanks.

From the **British Red Cross Society**, 26 December 1943:

Firstly I must thank you for your splendid show, and for the intense pleasure you gave the patients & Nursing Staff with the varied items they so enjoyed at the Wroxham Hall Red Cross Hospital. The patients were so overcome with your great generosity in bringing them cigarettes and candies saying nothing of the chewing gum! All so intriguing to them! So I have the patients' gratitude to express to you, as well as the above Society's heartfelt thanks to your kind men who never turn a request aside as we have proved, & for which we are deeply grateful.

From the **National Fire Services**, No.13 Fire Force Area, 24 January 1945:

I am very sorry that I did not see you on Sunday evening to say 'goodbye', but as the weather was bad for travelling we left immediately after the Concert.

Thank you very much for a most enjoyable evening. Your Officers were extremely kind to all of us, and personally I should like you to convey my thanks to Lieut. LeRoy.

**Leon Vance**'s story includes one moving incident relating to an English child: When he found out he had lost his foot, Vance alternated between a sort of ironic glee and fits of depression. During one of the depressed stages, he was crutching along a London street when an eight-year-old boy yelled at him 'You'll never miss it, Yank!'

'The kid's mother came up to me and apologized,' says Vance. 'Then she explained that he had lost his own foot in the blitz and was getting along fine with an artificial one. That was the biggest boost I got. Felt a devil of a lot better after that.'

# Chapter Ten

# Through English Eyes

Turning to the British viewpoint, there is an immediate difference in tone, partly due to the different nature of the sources. These are mainly spoken rather than written, a reminder of the importance of oral history for research into the twentieth century – and of the excellence of the Norfolk Sound Archive, part of the Norfolk Record Office.

The first time **Phyllis Smales** (née King) heard the word Yanks was when she was picking peas on a farm near Rackheath with her family. She heard that the rumour was that the Yanks were coming over. Her mother said, 'ooh yes, they came over in the last war, the Yanks', 'ooh well' she said, 'nice lot of young boys they were too!' Her father, who had been in the army in the First World War, commented, 'Bloody Yanks, they come in when it's half finished' – but he thought they were good boys as well. Later, they used to come to the farm and chat with him. On one occasion, they borrowed the farm horses and everyone went to Salhouse Broad, everyone holding on for dear life. The only drink was coca-cola, but Phyllis recalled it as a lovely occasion with everyone singing on the way back to Rackheath in the evening.

Many British people worked on the bases in a variety of roles, and had contacts with the Americans through this. **Jim Turner's** father worked on road widening preparations for Seething airfield. **Russell Gower** worked on electrical maintenance at Halesworth airbase, repairing the runways, replacing lights and marking out lines: 'our electrician was making his perks by manufacturing bracelets out of silver three-penny pieces: they were very popular with the Americans.'

**Freda Harper** was seventeen and training as a telegraphist with the Post Office. After the Americans arrived, she joined the American Red Cross, working on the base and helping in the canteen 'with the peanut butter'. She recalled that one of the main meals eaten was spam, beans and chips.

Phyllis Smales was just fifteen-and-a-half years old when she began to work for the American Red Cross Club at Rackheath. She lived at the base: 'everyone I met there, they were real gentlemen'. Due to the high wages at the base, she was earning more money each week than her father did!

**Dick Wickham** recalled the American Red Cross clubmobile which went around the bases every day, giving out free donuts and cigarettes. He used to make donuts after school for the clubmobile and was paid seven shillings a week. At weekends, he and his friends were allowed to go all around the bases on the clubmobile.

**Kenneth Smith**, eighteen when the war broke out, went into the RAF and was posted to Hardwick: he remembered that he could buy cigarettes at the PX on the base much cheaper than anywhere else.

**John Goldsmith** worked at Halesworth base, and recalled that he was the first person to make use of the dentist on the base!

Phyllis thought 'they were like Hollywood stars, with the uniforms and their accents.' They used a phrase she had not heard before, 'atta girl', meaning 'well done'. **Tony North** noted unusual words too: 'elevator' for 'lift' and 'zee' not 'zed'. Turner's first impressions were also differences in speech. Asked if he remembered any problems with language:

> Well, I think that went both ways, you know. I think we eventually cottoned on to some of their unusual sayings and they found out what we were talking about.
>
> One thing that sort of stands out is that if an American stopped and asked you a direction for somewhere, you'd explain to turn left, right and whatever, and then you'd probably end up – or some of the older people would end up – 'Well, you can't miss it.' They kind of adopted this saying – 'You can't miss it' – and, I don't know if you know much about the system they used to get the aircraft into formation? They used what they called an assembly ship, and the one at Seething was painted in yellow and black squares, and it was actually called 'You Can't Miss It'!
>
> As kids, we picked up like they used to say 'Buddy'. First of all they used to talk about a 'furlong'. What's a furlong? We knew a furlong was a measurement, they meant a week's holiday or a week's leave. And 'Guys', you know they'd call you 'Guys' and used to say 'Ma'am' and 'Mom' or whatever. Yeah and 'God damn' and 'son-of-a-bitch' and all this sort of stuff.

**Miriam Riches** and **Joyce Marsham** recalled that the Americans used to have jam and bacon together in one sandwich. Turner found that the Americans made friends at several levels, with children, with girls and also with local families

## Laundry

**John Archer**: 'My mother would do the laundry for one of them, and he would bring a tin of spam.'

**Dick Wickham** recalled his visits to the local base when he was a child:

> I used to take washing home for my mother to do. They used to say to me, 'Can your mother do me some washing' and I used to end up with about three kit bags on my back on this cycle. And she did it all, she said she had six brothers in the forces during the war all over the world and she'd like to think somebody was doing it for them.'

It is hard today to think how much work this involved:

Of course there was no washing machine, she had to do it by hand and I used to take it back, and they said, 'How much do we owe your mother?' and I said 'I don't know'. Mother said, 'No, no, don't worry about it.'

One Christmas, a great big American truck pulled up and an officer knocked on the door: the men brought in loads of boxes of fruit and food in appreciation of her doing the washing. She said 'Get rid of it - people we'll think we're on the black market!' In the end, she distributed the gifts around the other houses in the street.

# Children

**Denis Duffield** used to visit Wendling as a schoolboy:

> I either walked or rode my ramshackle bicycle there every Saturday and Sunday, or whenever it was possible to get to the airfield in time to watch the bombers returning from a mission. Some were badly battle-damaged, coming in with only three engines, making wheels-up landings, and so on. Soon after the 392nd Bomb Group arrived during the summer of 1943, I became friends with a young GI from Fairmont, West Virginia. Louis was a PFC (Private First Class), and a member of the Ground Staff base Defence of the airfield. He used to bring me sweets and chewing gum, and cigarettes, tinned food etc for my parents. He also brought me the US Forces weekly magazine *Yank* which I accumulated as time went by.

Shortly after D-Day in June 1944, a large number of 8th Air Force ground personnel were transferred into the US Army from their East Anglian bases and fought alongside American Army troops in France, Belgium, Luxemburg and Germany. Louis was one of those transferred and was severely wounded in action during the Allied advance into Germany in early 1945. Louis married Pamela, a seventeen-year-old English girl, and they went to America in the summer of 1945, setting up home in Fairmont. However

> Pamela became extremely homesick, tearful, couldn't adjust to the American way of life and was very unhappy. When she was expecting a baby she wanted to have the child in England. With great reluctance, Louis let her return to England alone after being assured of her return following the birth of their daughter. Sadly, Pamela didn't return to West Virginia.

John Archer was fourteen and still at school when the Americans arrived. He used to be a plane spotter, noting down the numbers on the tails. **Tony North** was another boy interested in aircraft; he thought most boys were. He recalled that it was impossible to get onto RAF bases because of the high security, but the Americans were generally much more relaxed, the guards often allowing him and his friends to get close: 'there were no signposts so you had to explore to find anything'.

**David Walpole** used to give the Base Marshall fresh eggs: 'that used to be my entrance ticket'.

*Above and below:* American generosity: a British boy enjoys a visit to Rackheath.

**Dick Wickham** and his friends were allowed by the guards to cycle into the base; the ground crews invited them into the aeroplanes. Wickham joined the ATC when he was just fourteen and got a ride on a B-24: 'they let me fly the thing!'

Turner recalled that 'we saw Americans as a packet of chewing gum or a bag of sweets coming down the road.'

## Girls

Russell Gower's sister went out with two Americans during the war, one an airman, the other from the army. Both were killed in the war. Turner, who lived at Mundham recalled that five or six local girls married servicemen. John Archer knew eleven girls from his village who married Americans from the bases.

Freda Harper had a friend based at Seething who used to fly to North Africa; He once brought her back oranges. He went missing. She used to go to dances at the Rackheath base. The Americans picked them up and took them home. You 'used to bang on the floor of the truck when you wanted them to drop you off.'

Miriam and Joyce used to go to Shipdham base on Thursday nights for dances and to serve behind the canteen. Joyce's mother used to chaperone them. The airmen used to come out of the base for dances, and there was never any trouble between them and other men. The dances would finish about eleven. Sometimes an ambulance would be pressed into service to take the girls home if there was no other transport!

The archive contains the memoir of one GI Bride, **Sybil Neale**, who married Billy Billings: 'The Radio was playing 'The Yanks Are Coming'. Mom said, 'Here comes trouble'.'

Sybil recalls the Americans arriving in Norwich in early 1942, 'Soon the city filled with trucks and men on leave. Best remembered as the Liberty Run.' In April 1943, the 56th Fighter Group moved to Horsham St Faith's and, in May, officers threw a party for the men at The Lido dance hall. Sybil's friend Connie, who she volunteered with to help local farmers harvest their tomato crops, was dating an American, John 'Red' Woods, and Sybil went with her, 'In the middle of the dance, the Air Raid sirens sounded and I had to leave my blind date Billy Billings and run to my Depot.' Billy was then sent to Biggin Hill and she did not see him again until a month later when they met at a Thanksgiving dinner at Halesworth. They were engaged at Christmas 1943 and married in June 1944.

Sybil saved nine months of clothing coupons to buy her wine-coloured wedding suit and Billy, who was working in aircraft recovery, brought her a parachute from a crashed plane to make a slip out of but, she recalled: 'The material was woven on a 45-degree angle and no matter how you cut it the slip hung down on one side.'

She recalls her wartime wedding day:

Billy had no official pass. Bill Greieg his buddy in the Orderly Room made one up to look official. Lt Joseph Gelsinger … drove Billy to the church in a jeep from Boxted Airdrome … that night we had fish and chips for dinner … In the morning Red picked

*This spread:* All three cartoonists had their own take on the endlessly-repeated words, 'Any Gum Chum?' (John van Acker, Ray Waters and Jack Preston)

him up in the Staff Car. A few weeks later the girls in the Red Cross Club at the base baked a wedding cake for Billy and me.

## Families

Archer remembered that the Americans were very family-orientated. Gower recalled that one American stayed weekends with them, a waist gunner named Pat. He died later in a mid-air collision. When Americans came back to Freda's, her mother would do a few sausage rolls, which they thought were great. Three Americans came round to Miriam's family for Christmas lunch.

Tony North recalled that local families more or less adopted the Americans. An engineer from Horsham used to come to his house at weekends and sometimes during the week over a period of about eighteen months: 'He wasn't a youngster, he was 30–35; he had a wife back in the States'. He would turn up with a duffel bag full of tins that the cook on the base gave him when he said he was spending the weekend away: 'she had no idea what was in those tins'. They always brought food so as not to use up the rations in the house where they were guests. One day the family were invited to the Horsham base, shown around and given dinner in the officers' mess: 'They were giving us things and we didn't know what they were, and how to eat it'.

Phyllis used to go around to a school friend's in the evenings. Two Americans, Don Snyder and Earl Keifer, would visit them. One night she and Snyder got lost returning to the airbase, which got him into trouble with the 'snowdrops' [Military Police, so named for their white helmets].

Many British children recalled the Christmas parties we have already mentioned. **Brian 'Joe' Webb** of Honingham recalled:

I would say the highlights were the Christmas Parties by the Americans at the Attlebridge Base known as the 466 Bomber Group. They would invite the boys from the Hall and the village back to their camp. The Yanks would send two or three trucks, which were the GMC 6-wheeler personal carriers with the racked seats in the back and the canvas top. You had to climb almost 5–6 feet to get into the back of the truck, and then we would be transported to the Attlebridge bomber base. After disembarking from the trucks, we would then be taken into an army billet and each one of us on entering would be given a picture book. The tables and benches would stretch the full length of the billet, completely covered in food and soft drinks for all of us to sit together as one happy family. On the tables was food I had never seen before – bananas, ice cream in different colours and butter (what was that for?). From there we walked a few yards to another billet, which was a cinema, and given candy and spearmint chewing gum before seeing a film, then finally time to go home in the army trucks. The Americans gave us several parties in the early 1940s.

**John Archer:** 'They used to send trucks down to pick kids up for the Christmas party and give out oranges.'

British children queue up to see Father Christmas: The girl going into the hut is Yvonne James.

**Dick Wickham** also recalled the trucks fetching schoolchildren to parties at the bases, especially at Christmas. **Tommy Dungar**, in his teens, was just a bit too old for the party:

> [1944] was the best Christmas for the schoolchildren from Rackheath since the war started. In the morning they were thrilled to bits when they were all shown over the B-24 'Slick Chick'. This was followed by a tea party in the Mess hall with Spam and dried eggs, ice cream, candy bars, oranges and chewing gum. What made it so special was the fact that it was the first oranges and ice cream most of the children had ever seen, as the War had been on for almost five years. What made the ice cream so special was the fact that it had been taken up to 25,000 feet in the bomb bay of the B-24 'Wabbit' to keep it frozen until it was needed. I remember feeling rather envious at the time, missing out and having to go to work.

## Pubs

**John Archer** recalled that the airmen would go to the local pub. The landlord would water down the beer, and 'of course they did short change them'. The kids might earn their candy as **Turner** recalled in connection with the Garden House pub in Mundham:

The kids would wait outside, in case American military policemen came in chasing those airmen who had sneaked out of the base illegally – 'Hi kids, let us know when the MPs [Military Police] are coming' – because we could look up then road and see their jeep coming down the road, so we did this and whenever the MPs came down we just opened the pub door and we just shouted 'Snowdrops!' … The old landlord would lift the lid on his counter and all the ones that didn't have a pass, they'd all file through into his living room, taking the beer with them.

**Dick Wickham** recalled that the airmen would cycle to the pub and then get too drunk to cycle back – they would walk home and a truck would come over the next day to pick up the bikes. One pilot was short and had a bike much too big for him; Wickham would help him up into the saddle. After a while Wickham no longer saw him. He had gone on a raid and never returned.

**Phyllis Smales** remembered them at the local pub near Rackheath, most wearing baseball caps. On one occasion two Americans took on the locals at poker and fleeced them – but then left the money there for them to spend on drinks. Once they all got tight and drove back to Rackheath singing loudly. She recalled that, because of the extended British summertime, it was still light when they got back.

## Entertainment

**Freda Harper** noted that the Americans were good dancers, teaching her how to jive, or to jitterbug. She had encounters with several stars. She recalled the evening that Glen Miller played at Attlebridge for example: she was involved in a minor car crash on the way and could not dance as she was stiff all over. She also encountered James Stewart:

> My grandparents lived in Cherry Lane off St George's Street … and my mother worked as a cashier at the cinema there at the time. These two Americans came past on their bikes and wolf whistled me, and I thought 'I've seen you somewhere before', and when I got in my mother just said, 'Jimmy Stewart just came in – sat up in the front circle'.

Hollywood actor James Stewart was in fact at the height of his acting career when he entered the military. He enlisted just days after winning an Oscar for his role in *The Philadelphia Story*. Arriving in England in November 1943, he became a squadron commander with the 445th Bomb Group at Tibenham. He was awarded the Distinguished Flying Cross just three months later, on the first day of Big Week. Shortly afterwards, in March 1944, he was transferred to Old Buckenham, becoming group operations officer of the 453rd Bomb Group.

On one occasion Phyllis Smales went on a day trip to Yarmouth with two Americans, one the Colonel's driver, Corporal Raymond West, and another girl: 'The cafés were few and far between but I know we did have chips, something with chips with everything

Lt-Col. Jimmy Stewart, Old Buckenham control tower.

of course, and I know it was set up lovely. One of the airmen pinched a small spoon as a souvenir.' The group then went on to two cinemas!

On another occasion she went 'up the city' with her friend a Maltese girl, Lillian Kirby, who was going out with one of the Rackheath airmen, Wilbert Richard:

I used to go with them to Norwich and we went to the Sampson and Hercules, and the first time I had ever been to a posh hotel. Ray went that time, we went to the Castle and here was me, like now, in little flat-heeled shoes and a little wartime coat which had a belt tied round it, which was all the fashion in them days, looking very frightened indeed. We went to the Castle Hotel and we had to queue up, and they were all high-ranking officers, hardly a GI to be seen, but these two had the money you see, that was the money they had. And so we stood in the queue, eventually got a meal there. I mean I was full, couldn't possibly eat another thing. What happened was we then went straight to the Bell Hotel and it had swing doors, no, revolving doors, and there was a black-out curtain, so, trust me, I went in, went all the way round and out again on the step. So they came to look for me and as he pushed me forward I got my finger stuck in the door, so of course they thought the end of the world had come. They were making a fuss and I was just shaking it, you see, everyone turned round at the bar, all these ladies in summer dresses looked me up and down – what have they

'Wings for Victory' parade outside Norwich City Hall, 13 November 1945.

Their first t-shirts!

brought in? And we went up a large staircase and the head waiter in black tails – and he bowed you know and led the way – found us a table and we had soup to start with, and rolls, and I was sat on the outside of the table and I kept daring to raise my eyes and look around. All the ladies all had fabulous hair-dos, jewellery, high-heeled shoes, evening gowns – and there was us just sitting there! And I'll never forget the time it took me to eat my plate of soup. But I've always remembered that because that was something to brag about when I got home!

Relations between the Americans and the locals are almost always the subject of fond memories that have lasted over the years. Twins **John and Brenda Spittle**, who grew up near Shipdham airbase, recalled that their mother and grandmother did laundry for the servicemen there. They were given chocolate, and one American serviceman sent them t-shirts on his return to the States. These were the first t-shirts they had ever seen!

Jim Turner: 'the relationship between the servicemen and England here has been one of the great friendships of the century.'

Freda put it more bluntly: 'lots of my friends married them, so they must have been all right.'

# Chapter Eleven

# The End

The war in Europe was obviously coming to an end by the spring of 1945, but here were still losses. The last B-24 from 2nd Air Division to be shot down was the *Black Cat*, 486 BG, lost near Regensberg in southeast Germany on 21 April 1945. Ten crewmen died, only two – bombardier Christ Manners and tail gunner Al Seraydarian – surviving. They were captured and held prisoner until the end of the war. On 7 May, the Germans surrendered. It was time to go home.

**Willis Marshall:**

I was still going into Norwich each day but all of a sudden this came to a screeching halt on about the 10th or 12th of May when everyone was restricted to the base. Of course, we knew something was up but didn't know what. I think on the 19th we were told to pack and that we would be heading out the next day. We took off the next day and landed at Valley, Wales. With one night there we headed to Iceland … After a night in Iceland we loaded up, taxied out, checked engines and entered onto the runway. I remember looking down the runway. It seemed fairly long but seemed to have several dips and humps in it. That old war bird creaked and groaned as we gathered speed and as this was attained, Ken pulled back on the control column and we lifted off but settled right back down on the runway. With a short run Ken tried again, with the same results. We were fast running out of runway so Ken pulled us off a third time and this time that bird decided to fly. As we left the end of the runway I saw a pole of stones was piled between it and a cliff that dropped into the sea. We barely cleared that pile, for the guys standing in the bomb bay said that they could have reached down and snatched a stone off the top of that pile.

They flew to Goose Bay, Labrador that day and on the following day were back 'in the good old USA' arriving at Windsor Locks Connecticut: 'there were literally hundreds and hundreds of returned planes parked there'.

Even on the journey home there were some tragedies, such as that of the B-24 bomber of R. D. Ketchum of 44 BG, which crashed at Gairloch in Scotland after taking off from Prestwick. The nine crew members and six passengers were all killed. There is a plaque on the hillside that records their names.

At last the war was over and peace came back to East Anglia after six long years of war. As Ruth Sadlier wrote to Ivy Royal:

> It certainly must be a wonderful feeling to know that you can go to bed in peace and comfort and not have to sit up all hours of the nite and take the children out of their beds and worry and wonder where was going to get hit next. I feel so sorry for all the dear little children. It is so sad because I suppose their future lives will be affected by this terrible war. Why it has to be I never can guess. It certainly is a shame to see so many lives taken and ruined.

Even before the end of the war, thoughts had turned to ways to remember the fallen. **Rudolph Howell:**

> I guess it's no military secret to tell you that the second air division (my division) is planning to erect a memorial in the nearest large town (I wish I could say what the town is). It is to be something in the order of an annex to the proposed new public library. It will cost £20,000 (I'm pretty sharp on this English money), which is a neat sum. I plan to contribute one pound. As you have no doubt gathered we of the second air division are having to pay for the memorial ourselves, but strangely enough I am of the opinion that it will be worthwhile. It will have a Roll of Honor of all those killed in our division, and some busts of our big wheels etc. But what I like most of all is that it will have an individual short history of each group.

A leaflet was produced to promote the appeal:

> The Flame Must Burn On!

> When the last bomb has been dropped, the last shot fired; when the winds aloft have washed the last traces of this holocaust from the skies, we who are left will go home. As some returning soldier so aptly put it: 'If the Statue of Liberty wants to see me again, she'll have to turn around!'
>
> But what of those whom we must leave here? We all have memories of gallant comrades who paid the supreme sacrifice in war-torn hostile skies and those who died honourably in line of duty. In order to perpetuate their memory, we propose to erect a Memorial to those honoured dead – *your* memorial to *them*. The Memorial must be a spiritually living thing. The deep and sacred feeling giving birth to this Memorial, their spirit of youth, hope, and desire for a world of decency, freedom, and peace must live on – must imbue this Memorial with that same sacred spirit dedicated to oncoming generations whose way of life they died to protect. The Memorial must be a haven wherein the flame of their principles must burn brightly and eternally, wherein the bewildered, stumbling footsteps of succeeding generations can be unerringly placed on the right paths.
>
> For those who have paid the supreme sacrifice, and for whom there can be no permanent resting place, such a Memorial to their families and friends will represent

tangible living evidence of the heart-felt gratitude and love of their country and comrades with whom they lived and thought – for when the airfields are plowed up, and all vestiges of the chaos of war have disappeared in time, this will remain a perpetual tribute to their memory – to their faith in an ideal.

Major General Kepner added his own message, which can be seen on the following page.

The plans underwent many changes before the formal dedication of the Memorial Library on 13 June 1963. A special message from President Kennedy was read out:

> On the Occasion of the Dedication of this Memorial, I would like to join in paying tribute to the six thousand members of the Second Air Division who sacrificed their lives in the defense of free men everywhere.
>
> These men and their companions in arms in the Royal Air Force and the United States Army Air Corps were given the hard task of risking the present for the future. They met the test. May their sacrifice continue to strengthen the bonds of friendship between our two nations, allies past and present, against tyranny. May it also inspire us to pursue with energy and patience the opportunities for securing peace with justice preserved for us by those whose memorial we dedicate today.

The Memorial Room held the divisional Roll of Honor, which contained the names of almost 7,000 men who lost their lives while serving with the Division. It also held the book stock of books on American history and culture. In the courtyard outside, a memorial fountain featured a mosaic using a stone from each of the fifty states of the union. Twenty years later, in 1983, representations of the Division's bomber and fighter units' aircraft colours and a large photographic mural were added.

On 1 August 1994, the Central Library building burned down. The Memorial Room book stock and the Roll of Honor were destroyed in the blaze. A new Library was built and a new 2nd Air Division Memorial Library has been included, providing almost double the space of the room destroyed in the 1994 fire. The new library room was dedicated on 7 November 2001.

Many Americans have donated material to the Memorial Library, and many others have given it financial support. The Jordan Uttal and Evelyn Cohen Trust has enabled the archive to be properly catalogued and made available to the public. Both played their part in the war. Jordan Uttal enlisted in the United States military following the attack on Pearl Harbour, December 1941, and arrived in Norfolk in May 1943. He was stationed at 2nd Air Division Headquarters, obtaining the rank of Major by the end of his military service, and had overall responsibility for statistical data, including bombing accuracy analysis. In December 1944, Uttal married Joyce Christie King, a British Civilian Assistant with the Red Cross, at City Hall, Norwich. After the Second World War, Jordan returned to America with Joyce and worked in the American food industry. Jordan Uttal was also a founder of the 2nd Air Division Association for veterans. He served the Association for over sixty-two years and was its Honorary President from 1989.

## HEADQUARTERS 2d AIR DIVISION
### APO 558

To The Men of 2d Division :

*The plan for the erection of a memorial to the men of 2d Division who have given their lives for their country has, I know, a universal appeal. All of us have friends and comrades who have been lost in action against the enemy or who have died in performance of their duty as American soldiers. These are the hard and bitter facts of war. These men live in our memory not only because of our sense of personal loss but also because of the admiration and respect we have for them and for the supreme sacrifice which they have made for their country and for their comrades. Their loss has been even more deeply felt by their loved ones at home to whom they will never return.*

*This memorial will be a shrine to which the families and loved ones of these gallant comrades, and indeed many of us, may return in years to come. It will be in every way worthy of the men whose memory it perpetuates and of the cause for which they gave their lives. The stately and beautiful hall of memory will furnish a harmonious setting for the Group plaques to be placed on its walls and for the bound volumes containing Group histories and the Group Rolls of Honor. More than that, however, it will be a memorial of living spiritual significance for, through the American Reference Library and the American Reading Room, it will bring a daily influence of American thought and ideals to the people of the Norwich community with whom we have been so closely associated during these difficult years.*

*I know that all of you will welcome this opportunity to express in concrete form what so many of you already have in your minds, and the collection of the sum required will not be difficult if the response is as enthusiastic as I expect it to be.*

*Together we have built the 2d Division into one of the greatest aerial striking forces in history. Together let us build this fitting memorial to its officers and men who have sacrificed their lives to overthrow the enemies of our country in order that the ideals of our American democracy, and indeed all democracy, shall endure.*

W. E. KEPNER,
*Major General, USA*
Commanding

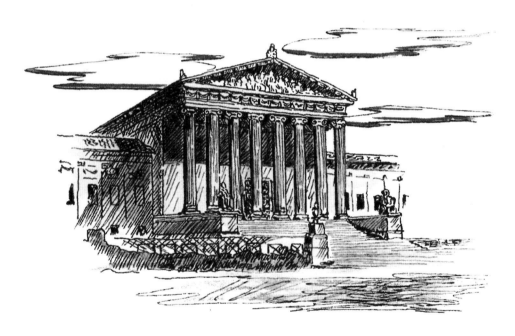

NORWICH, ENGLAND
1945

Evelyn Cohen served with the WACs at Ketteringham Hall, and played a major role in the 2nd Air Division Association after the war. Many British people have also given much of their time in support of the Memorial Library, especially T. D. 'Tom' Eaton, who served on the Trust for well over thirty years as Governor, Vice-Chairman and Chairman, and whose dedication played a major role in seeing the project through to its completion. The American Memorial Library has become, as intended, the centre of links between the peoples of East Anglia and the United States.

Other memorials include museums at bases such as Hethel and Seething, and plaques in or near the bases and at the sites of individual crashes. American serviceman and women who died in the war are remembered at the Madingley American cemetery, near Cambridge, which contains the graves of 5,800 of the dead, and is the only American Second World War Cemetery in the United Kingdom. It was established as a temporary cemetery in 1943 and formally dedicated as a permanent military cemetery on 16 July 1956. Memorial Day ceremonies are held at the cemetery every year on the last Monday in May.

The final word should rest with the servicemen and women themselves. Even at the time, many airmen appreciated the way in which they were received in East Anglia. **An unnamed American airman** wrote to a Norfolk family in 1945: 'It would seem superficial if I were to try and thank you for all you did for me while I was in England because I feel that you realize what your kindness meant to me. I shall always feel that you are one of my real friends even though we only knew each other a short while and

Inside the American Memorial Library.

TO THE MEMORY OF THE
UNDERMENTIONED MEMBERS OF
753ᴿᴰ SQUADRON 458ᵀᴴ BOMB GROUP
2ᴺᴰ BOMBARDMENT DIVISION U.S.A.A.F
WHO DIED NEAR THIS SPOT
24ᵀᴴ NOVEMBER 1944

THE PILOT OF THE BOMBER AS HIS
LAST ACT AVOIDED CRASHING ON
THIS AND SURROUNDING COTTAGES
THUS PREVENTING THE POSSIBLE
LOSS OF CIVILIAN LIVES

2/LT. RALPH J. DOOLEY, PILOT. 744 E. ONTARIO STREET, PHILADELPHIA, PA.
2/LT. ARTHUR AKIN JR. PILOT. 92 WALLACE CIRCLE, PORTSMOUTH, VA.
2/LT. PAUL E. GORMAN, NAVIGATOR. 2542 E. 29ᵀᴴ ST. BROOKLYN, N.Y.
S/SGT. JOHN J. JONES, WAIST GNR. GENERAL DELIVERY, GEM, TEXAS.
S/SGT. PAUL A. WADSWORTH, RADIO OPERATOR. BOX 655, FORSAN, TEXAS.
S/SGT. OSCAR B. NELSON, BALL TURRET GUNNER. VASHON, WASH.
S/SGT. JOHN A. PHILLIPS, ENGINEER. NORTH MAIN ST. NORWOOD NORFOLK NJ
S/SGT. DONN P. QUIRK, TAIL GUNNER. MUNCIE, IND.
S/SGT. RALPH VON BERGEN, WAIST GUNNER. 507 LIPAN ST DENVER, COLO.

Heigham street memorial.

Memorial in Hethel churchyard.

I hope that you feel the same about me.'

Many others thought the same:

**John Rex:**

The success of the 2nd Air Division was due, in no small part, to the people of East Anglia for they received us in friendship and they did go out of their way to try and make it as comfortable for us as possible ... The folks of East Anglia must know that we know it was a great team effort, and they were a major part of that effort.

**William Head:** 'the whole-hearted acceptance of Americans was the greatest gift the people of Norfolk could give us. They shared their pubs with us, invited us into their homes, gave us fresh eggs, washed our laundry. They made some very sad and 'lost' airmen feel at home.'

**Mary Williams-Elder:**

The people over here are so friendly and so different from what I have always heard of the English people. I always thought of them as very reserved and hard to get along with, but they are exactly the opposite. They come up to you and invite you to their homes, ask you questions about the states and are just as friendly as can be.

The 'friendly invasion' had an enormous effect on many people living in East Anglia at the time.

It affected the young Americans too. In the words of **James Caulfield:** 'Once you go to England, you never come all the way back.'

# Chapter Twelve

# Lest We Forget

The past is recorded in many ways: in diaries and journals, made at the time, in later reminiscences, and in photography and artwork: all of these have been used in this book. At least one published poet has played his part: Hyam Plutzik, born in Brooklyn in 1911. His parents were Jews who had emigrated to the United States from what is now Belarus. He enlisted and served at Shipdham in the last year of the war as an Ordinance Officer, later as Education and Information Officer. He published several books of poems after the war, including the book-length poem *Horatio* on which he had worked while at Shipdham. A number of his shorter poems relate to his time at Britain, such as 'The Airman Who Flew Over Shakespeare's England', 'Bomber Base' and 'On the Airfield at Shipdham'.

> The runways stretch silent; somewhere in the blackness
> The guards stand, unseen, longing for home,
> And a woman's arms, a warm bed in a house
> (from 'Bomber Base')

He describes the planes as:

> The beasts with guts of metal groaning on the line
> Or in the higher sky solemnly muttering
> (from 'On the Airfield at Shipdham')

Plutzik died in 1962. His *Collected Poems* were published in 1987: they deserve to be better known in England.

Between 1942 and 1945, there were as many as 50,000 American men and women within 30 miles of Norwich, with an airfield approximately every 5 miles. This is hard to imagine in today's Norfolk. As the years pass, many of the bases of the 2nd Air Division are no longer visible on the ground, having reverted to agricultural use or become housing estates. However, each base has its own memorial. A number of enthusiastic volunteers have set up museums to preserve the reality of life on an airbase for present and future generations. Seething control tower and the chapel/gymnasium building at Hethel are now museums for 448 BG and 389 BG: Hethel also incorporates

The former chapel at Hethel airbase
(*below*) and the control tower at
Seething (*left*) are both now museums.

material from 466 BG based at Attlebridge. There are other airbase museums at Halesworth, where both 489 BG and 56 FG were based, at Shipdham (44 BG), at Hardwick (93 BG), and aviation museums at Horsham St Faith and Flixton, Bungay. All these are excellent places to recall the events of the war as played out in the fields of East Anglia. As we have seen, the 2nd Air Division American Memorial Library is also dedicated to making sure that the aspect of the Second World War described in this book is remembered, and that links between East Anglia and the United States are promoted in every possible way: it is truly a living memorial.

Almost 6,900 young Americans from the 2nd Air Division gave their lives defending the cause of freedom: their story must never be forgotten.